NOW YOU ARE MARRIED

A Practical Guide for Love Birds Who Desire a Happy Home

ODY ADEDE AGBOR

ISBN: 978-978-972-780-3

DEDICATION

To couples who want to experience heaven on earth in a godly and blissful marriage.

ACKNOWLEDGEMENT

I am grateful to God Almighty, the ultimate source of my
inspiration.

Words are not enough to appreciate my beloved husband,
Mr. Matthew Agbor, for his support, understanding and love
throughout this book project.

I also want to appreciate my loving parents, Dr. Nkanu Eja
Bassey and Mrs Margaret Bassey,my amiable parents in-law,
Mr. & Mrs. Victor Agbor, and the wonderful members of my
extended/nuclear family. You all are the best team anyone
could ever wish for.

I appreciate Mrs. Rose-Ann Oyama for writing the foreword
of this book and for her love, care and advice. .

In no small measure, I appreciate the professional editing
skills of my editor, Eno Sam, founder of Brilliant Writers
Academy.

I appreciate the staff and students of Elder Oyama Memorial
group of schools, Cross River, Nigeria.

To my spiritual parents and amazing friends, I appreciate
your support and love.

To my dear readers, thanks for getting a copy of my book. I believe that this book will help you build a godly marriage.

FOREWORD

I am filled with joy, happiness and praise to God as I remember my little Ody. I watched her grow from a curious little girl to a vivacious young woman filled with a God- given passion and zeal to share knowledge and wisdom with all.

Now You Are Married is not only timely and needed for newly married couples but also for those who have been married for long. This piece of work is light hearted and full of wisdom for those who want to get married and stay happily married.

I have known many who decided to get married with little or no knowledge of what is expected of them. This book serves as an eye opener and a valid tool to help newly married couples and old couples who have fallen into bad habits. If married couples can yield themselves to the Lordship of God, the Holy Spirit will give them great insight into understanding what the creator of marriage intended it to be. Ody has efficiently dealt with the most pertinent topics for successful marriages and relationships in this book. Every couple needs to read it together and enjoy the blessings that await them. This is the go-to book for married people.

It is my prayer that as you read this book, you would not only grow stronger in your walk with the Lord but you would also get closer in unity and love with each other.

Mrs. Rose-Ann Oyama
Author, My Spouse, My Friend.
Canada.

CONTENTS

INTRODUCTION

A lot of young couples get married with thoughts that it's the beginning of a fairy tale but few months or years into the marriage, they are confused about so many things. They do not know who to talk to; some do but are afraid of it being the topic of discussion the next day. Somehow, they start seeing marriage as a scam and set-up. Those who grew up witnessing terrible marriages which they wished never to experience are already discouraged with what they are seeing in their own marriage and have given up secretly in their hearts saying, "No one is really enjoying their marriage. No wonder married people laugh when they see beautiful pre-wedding pictures and say welcome to the 'club' with sarcasm in their voice." Some newly married couples think within themselves. What about that young lady who got married a virgin and hasn't been able to conceive yet and is worried with several visits to the gynaecologist. Some are so scared because nobody told them that can happen. All they heard was, "In nine months, we will come visiting." What about the young married woman who cries at night, fighting for her husband's affection, love and attention with a strange woman? Should she give up and call marriage a scam like most people do? What about the subtle things that kill joy in marriage which most young couples are not aware of.

NOW YOU ARE MARRIED is not just a random book but a practical guide for young couples who have walked down the aisle. In this book, you will find answers to most disturbing questions on the minds of young couples. I sincerely hope that this book would help you survive the new years of your marriage and beyond. Together with your spouse, do the exercises at the end of each chapter for maximum effectiveness. It's worthy of note that this book is a sequel to my first relationship book titled, Before You Get Married.

CHAPTER ONE

ADJUSTING TO A NEW LIFE/STATUS

Congratulations on getting married; it is such a beautiful experience especially if you are married to the one God kept for you until it was time. However, after the wedding comes the marriage and for those who did not co-habit, it would be a time to start living together as husband and wife. This would demand many adjustments from both parties. When the lady was single, she could cook only when she felt like, wake up at any time and prepare for work or her daily activities but as a married woman, she needs to wake up a bit earlier than usual and start planning meals that should be cooked. This is not to say the man should not help out in cooking when he can or if he enjoys cooking.

The man will also have to adjust his numerous outings and hanging out late with 'the boys' knowing his wife is waiting for him at home. It was not like that before he got married. As a bachelor, he could stay out late and spend the night at his friend's house and not be bothered but marriage requires that he informs his wife if he has to stay out late due to an official engagement or other personal needs. This is where many men miss it. They feel their wives are trying to control them and so they revolt, "How can you tell me when to come back home? I can come back anytime I like. Do you think you can control me? Marriage is not bondage." You are very correct about marriage not being bondage but it is common sense to know that every class needs a new curriculum. You cannot do in SS1 what you did while you were in JSS1. It can't work that way. The same rule applies with marriage. Those things that worked out perfectly well when you were still single cannot apply in marriage.

I have found out that this is usually the beginning of marital issues for newly married couples. Either or the both of them are not ready to adjust to their new status/life. For some people, this adjustment comes naturally and easily while it takes time for others to finally adjust. For some others, it has not yet dawned on them that they are now married and therefore, some things cannot remain the same.

Let me share my personal experience with you.

Before I got married, whenever my husband-to-be visited my parents, he would stay in the guest room while I sleep in my sister's room or alone in my room. We could come to the parlour and discuss for as long as we wanted to but when it was time to retire to bed, he would go to the guest room while I would go to my room. Precisely a week after our wedding, we visited our parents' house to thank the church over there for their support during our wedding ceremony and something funny happened. After eating, I waved to my husband and was moving to my room. My mother quickly asked me to stay with my husband in the guest room. That was when it dawned on me that I was really married and needed to adjust my previous courtship attitude each time we visit my parents together. I would have to stay in the guest room with my husband except I visit alone.

When I was still single, I once heard a marriage counsellor admonish married couples to spend at least one year living alone without anybody but I couldn't really understand the need for that. Having been married for years, I now understand. As two different people from different backgrounds (cultural, social, educational etc) come together to form a union, there is bound to be adjustment. Having people in the house already with the couple can make this quite difficult especially for some family members who are yet to understand that their son or daughter is now married. They are yet to come to terms with that; so they feel they can still make critical decisions for them.

For instance, a young wife cooks for her husband and unknown to her, the food is salty. If the husband's mother is there and she is the type that magnifies things, she can make a mountain out of this. She might start making the young woman feel very uncomfortable and that is the last thing a new wife wants. Possessive in-laws can make it hard for a new couple to adjust.

Marriage is not a burden. It has its own rules and these rules must be obeyed if one wants a happy home. Marriage bestows honour on you. Therefore, it is expected of married couples to act honourably. That's why people often say, "he/she is not behaving like a married man/woman" when they see married people acting irresponsibly. You need to adjust the time you spend outside as well. You must realize you are not only responsible for yourself but for someone else too. You cannot just wake up in the morning and tell your spouse you are leaving town for a meeting. Your partner should be informed early enough to help him/her prepare his/her mind except it is an emergency.

As a single lady, I could care less if there was no food at home but now, I am so conscious of the fact that there has to be food. This is why some people believe one should cut off from single friends. Well, I don't believe in that philosophy unless they are bad influence to your marriage. A very good friend of mine who is still single invited me to her city and before she ended the conversation, she said, "You have to confirm from Mr. Matthew if the time is okay with him." I was happy she understood that I can't just wake up and leave my home without his consent. Just before some people who feel the woman becomes a slave after marriage misinterpret this, let me state here that my husband seeks my consent always before travelling anywhere.
The other day, I was out with a friend who was not yet married at that time and the outing took a longer time than planned. I politely had to tell her that we have to round off

quickly to enable me hurry home to prepare a meal for my husband before he gets back home. At first, she asked, "Can't he cook for himself?" I told her that he can do that, after all he was doing that before we got married, but it gives me joy to serve his meals especially after he has been away at work. Moreover, I was off work that week and he should enjoy me being around. Something as little as your sleeping pattern might also need an adjustment. I was someone who didn't like my night sleep being interrupted by anyone because naturally, I hardly get to sleep within the day and so once I sleep in the evening, I do not like to be disturbed at all. However, that changed after my wedding. It took me a while to adjust but after a while, I got used to it.

Before we discuss few areas that new couples need to make adjustments, it's crucial to emphasize that bad manners should not be overlooked until marriage. Your single days should be spent grooming yourself and improving your character. Marriage is neither an escape route nor a place to start behaving responsibly. Be keen about being responsible even before you walk down the aisle. The points listed below are key things to consciously adjust once you're married.

Personal Space

As minute as this adjustment is, it can cause a lot of issues. Each person might be coming from a background where they had a room to themselves or had a very big family house; others lived alone immediately after their studies at the university. Depending on the couple's financial level, their new house might be smaller than what they were used to. Now, you need to share a bed with someone else everyday, especially for couples who do not believe in the idea of separate rooms. If you are the type that is so used to being alone, you have to adjust. Some people can roll over the bed different times before morning. You have to be careful while doing that so you don't end up hitting the other person's eyes, nose or head in the process. Nevertheless, the good news is that you will adjust in this area soon.

Adjusting to In-laws

The truth is that in Africa, marriage is still a family thing. Once you get married, you need to adjust to accommodate your in-laws as well. The wife cannot expect the husband to fully embrace her family members while she does the opposite. As the man, when you are planning to reach out to your family, you should try to reach out to your wife's family too. Based on my observation, this is what causes serious disagreements especially in African marriages. One spouse expects the other to welcome his/her family members into the home and the other frowns and gets irritated when the family members of his/her spouse sends a message that they plan visiting them. The husband releases money to get everything once his parents inform him of their visit but constantly complains of being broke when his wife informs him of her parents' visit. The wife makes proper preparation and turns into a chef automatically, cooking all type of meals in preparation to welcome her parents but will not care if there is food to offer her husband's parents. In as much as marriage is a couple thing, we cannot overlook the fact that everyone once had a family before marriage. The family of orientation (that is the family a person is born into) is also as important as the family of procreation (the family formed through marriage and child birth). The only thing needed is wisdom on how to balance the two. No one should suffer at the expense of the other.

A new couple should adjust to accommodate the presence of in-laws. I do not mean accommodating them in one's home alone but knowing that you now have an additional new family.

Financial Adjustment

Before you got married, you could be the one that spends on impulse. Most people with the sanguine personality fall under this category because they are fun lovers. As a husband, you cannot afford to buy everything you see. You need to prioritize your needs especially if your income isn't on the high side. New couples have to make serious adjustment in this area if their income is extremely low. You are now thinking of building a home together and finance is needed for many things in marriage.

As a married man, you cannot decide to send all your savings to your family of orientation except there is an urgent need.

Even at that, it should be done with the consent of your spouse. Most couples decide to operate joint accounts after marriage. If this is what you want, you are free to do so.

As a man, you should be able to cater for your family. Even if your wife earns more than you, that isn't an excuse to delegate all the duties to her. Agreement must have been made before getting married. The man should be able to take care of the main things needed to run the home smoothly while the wife can take care of some petty expenses in the home when necessary. As a wife, be willing to assist your husband when he is financially down.

That brings us to the question I've heard new couples ask. **Should we operate a joint account?** Most new couples asking this question have already made up their mind on what to do. I am not here to tell you what to do with your finances. I can only offer suggestions and leave it open for you to decide.

I have always believed in having a single account as well as a joint account. That way, you can decide to put a percentage of your income to your individual account and another percentage to the joint account. You still enjoy the benefits of a joint account and maintain some sort of financial freedom.

The Institute for Marriage and Family Affairs (TIMFA) recommends joint account for married couples as it is no longer 'my money' but 'our money' and the argument is this, "If we share our bodies, why can't we share our money?" This doesn't stop you from spending to get what you need because the both of you get what is called play money. This helps you gain access to money when it is needed and keep track of expenditures. Both parties have to sit down and discuss extensively on this. You must be truthful to each other and not cheat the other person by spending money out of this account carelessly. This is usually what makes a lot of couples kick against it.

If you decide to operate a different account as a man, it's advisable to put your wife's name or children's name as the next of kin. You are now married and your family should come first. No one is praying for sudden death but make sure your family is financially protected and won't have to suffer especially for men who insist their wives remain housewives until they have finished child bearing. As a man gets married, he should think of his family of procreation in any financial decision he makes. Unfortunately, most married men still use the names of their sisters, brothers or cousins as their next of kin in their bank accounts.

There was a popular doctor who was shot and had to undergo a major surgery while unconscious in the hospital for weeks. The wife ran to his account officer asking for a release of 4 million naira for the operation immediately. The account officer said, "Madam, you are not the next of kin. So I can't release such an amount to you." She soon realized that none of her kids were the next of kin. The husband used his younger sister who was nowhere to be found. The man died and his sister took all the money (over 24million naira), leaving nothing for his wife and children. Obviously, the man and his wife had not been getting along financially. As a man, know that your wife comes first before your sister or brother.

In summary, sit together as a couple and choose an accounting system that you know will work for both of you, not necessarily the one you are most comfortable with. Remember that successful people do the right thing, not the comfortable thing.

Accommodate Each Other's Personality

Before we look into this, let's examine the different personality traits. Even though there are many personality traits, we shall focus on just four for the purpose of this book: Sanguine, Phlegmatic, Choleric and Melancholic.

— Sanguine Temperament

People with sanguine personality like to be around people, are easily amused, lively, carefree, love adventure and are poor at coping with boredom. It is also worthy to note that they are pleasure seeking individuals and might find it hard to remain on tasks. Being expressive, they talk a lot. However, they can be creative and fantastic entertainers.

— Phlegmatic Temperament

People with this personality are loyal, love to preserve their relationships and avoid conflicts. They look for ways to act as a mediator between people who might be fighting to restore peace. They are calm and easy going and tend to be in control of their emotions. It won't be wrong if they are termed the most peaceful and stable of all temperaments. It is quite difficult for people with the phlegmatic temperament to have any type of addiction.

— Choleric Temperament

People with the Choleric temperament are usually analytical and logical. They do enjoy deep and meaningful discussions and will choose to be alone than being with people with shallow mindset. They are firm in their approach and strive to lead. People with this temperament are not easily discouraged.

— Melancholic Temperament

People who fall under this temperament prefer long held traditions and love their families and friends. They do not necessarily look out for fun or adventure; contrary to some belief that they are not social beings, they can be social but extremely orderly and accurate and as such, they do well in managerial positions. Their ability to look critically at a situation and view it from all sides makes them good problem solvers.

People can have two temperament types; the primary and the other secondary. I know you might be wondering how the inability to adjust and understand your spouse's temperament can cause an issue in your marriage. Let's study this example.

A husband might have the choleric temperament and his wife the sanguine temperament. Remember that one of the characteristics of the choleric is that they enjoy deep and meaningful discussions. The husband with choleric temperament might find it hard to understand why his wife with sanguine temperament enjoys talking a lot; even things that he considers senseless. If he doesn't understand that his wife is wired that way, he might start feeling irritated and wonder why the wife cannot stay on a project for long without him having to remind her but she has no difficulty in discussing for hours and making friends easily.

You won't also get angry when your sanguine wife wants to have fun at all times and keep showing you various tourist sites that can be visited. Also, a husband with the sanguine personality will love to spend at impulse and take hasty spending decisions while his melancholic wife would want to analyse what is to be bought critically and try to view the investment from all sides. If he doesn't understand his wife's temperament, he might see her as too slow and wouldn't mind calling her the enemy of his progress in the heat of anger.

This is why it is important to understand the different temperaments. If he understands his wife is just being careful, instead of calling her a snail; he would try to convince her that the investment is for their own good and that he has gone through the whole terms/conditions of the investment and it is such a good offer that they can't afford to miss.

When you see your phlegmatic wife telling you to make peace with your perceived enemy, you will understand that she is doing that because of her temperament, not because she just wants to irritate you or isn't on your side.

That isn't to say adjustment can't be made in areas you see as extreme; it can be made but you have to lovingly draw your spouse's attention. Note here that my emphasis is on extreme cases. You probably feel embarrassed when you go for a function and your wife is so loud; it's as if she is the only one there and you find it very embarrassing that everyone tends to be hearing only her voice. You might also not like it that she spends on impulse. You give her money for a month's upkeep and at the end of the first week, she is already on your neck for additional money. You have to look for ways to relate with her to avoid constant strife. You might have to consider giving her money for weekly upkeep as against monthly upkeep if you have talked and spoken to her on the issue and it doesn't seem to be yielding any positive result. Remember, the Bible says that we should dwell with ourselves according to wisdom.

Love Birds Exercise 1.

• Now you're married, what adjustments would you make henceforth?

• What are the areas that are taking you time to adjust to?

• What other areas do you think you still need adjustment?

• Write down top things to do daily for your marriage success. Start doing them.

• Have you been able to understand your temperament and that of your spouse?

• If you're single, prepare your mind for the various adjustments in this chapter.

CHAPTER TWO

THE POWER OF UNITY

This chapter is very dear to my heart for two major reasons. Firstly, I didn't have this under my original outline but when I got done with chapter one and wanted going to the next chapter, this aspect dropped in my spirit. I resisted the urge initially but I remembered that I prayed before I commenced writing this book and one of my prayers was, "Lord, let me write all you want me to write, not what I feel like writing."

Secondly, I remember an experience that almost took my life barely two weeks after I got married and I knew that one of the things that saved me from the cold hands of death was the fact that my husband and I were spiritually united before that demonic attack. Apart from our family members and very few close friends, this story I am about to share has been kept private. I had a strong leading to share this story for the benefit couples in general, not just new couples. The words in Amos 3:3 are very important in the aspect of marriage, "Can two walk together except they be agreed?"

THE EXPERIENCE THAT NEARLY TOOK MY LIFE

After we got married, we immediately left for our honeymoon. Our first stop was Obudu Cattle Ranch located in Cross River State and after that, we left for the nation's capital, Abuja. After spending few days there, we decided to come back to Cross River and we agreed to stop over at my village to thank the people for their support during our wedding before heading to our permanent house in Calabar.

That morning before we left Abuja, my husband led us in prayers and I noticed he kept cancelling the spirit of death. I could not understand his reason for that but I said amen repeatedly. We had a smooth journey since he was the one driving and so, he was careful. In fact, the journey was fast and memorable. I can remember vividly that as soon as we got to a junction in my former local government, a text message dropped in his phone. I quickly looked and saw the sender's name; it was a female's name. I decided to get the phone to enable me read the message but he refused and asked why I was so inquisitive about seeing the content of the message. Before and after we got married, he hadn't given me any reason to doubt or suspect him and even to date, I don't know why I was so eager to read that text message.

I suddenly started making a scene out of it and he allowed me read the message. The sender was just wishing him happy new month and congratulating him on his marriage.

After that, I suggested that we get snacks at a nearby supermarket. He obliged and asked me to get the things alone. Again, I flared up thinking he was still upset about the text message incident without knowing that he was not himself.

We finally got home and I don't know who initiated the idea of praying together but I am happy we did apologize to each other and prayed. Little did we know that we were about to experience the first spiritual attack ever in our marriage. I exchanged pleasantries, ate my food and as I entered the bathroom to have a shower, I slummed. Thankfully, I was able to call the attention of my husband when I sensed something was wrong with me. For over four hours, I laid unconscious. I thank God for my parents who immediately understood that it was a spiritual attack and didn't rush me to the hospital. If they did, I would have been pronounced dead. I was told that they called more ministers of God and they waged spiritual warfare against the powers of darkness. God ministered to my husband to breathe the breath of life into me. He did that and I jerked back to life, vomiting and totally weak.

As soon as I was stabilized, life started going out of my husband. I now had to stand on the legal ground of being his wife and spoke life into him. To cut the long story short, God gave us complete victory. When we got a little strong to talk, he told me that before we left Abuja, he had a scary dream; he saw both of us dead and placed in a coffin.

The enemy needed us to be in disunity for that dream to see the light of day. Little wonder, he got us arguing, shouting and quarrelling during the journey. He told me he couldn't stop at the supermarket as he didn't understand himself at all because he felt strange in his body. I don't want to imagine what would have happened to us if we were not in unity. Maybe it would have been a totally different story. I am so glad that I learnt the power in unity very early in my marriage.

 Unity is not just saying with your mouth that you are united whereas your heart is so far apart. It is being united in spirit as well. It is being sensitive in the spirit and not allowing the enemy to rent a space in your home. As a couple, you should be spiritually sensitive to know when the devil just wants to gain access to your home by bringing up an argument to keep you and your spouse divided.

A young Christian lady once told us that whenever she is ovulating, there must always be an argument and serious misunderstanding between her husband and herself. At times, it will get so heated that they would end up sleeping in separate rooms for days and completely avoid sex but as soon as she is no longer ovulating, they will get back together and be so much in love.

The good thing was that she opened up to her pastor and he told her to refuse being at war at that time no matter how much the urge was. She understood spiritual matters more and decided that she was going to be more alert and sensitive. Today, she has all her children.

At the time you are meant to spend planning your future together as a couple, the enemy can just make the man's ex or the lady he fell into sexual sin with in the past to call him. A wife who isn't spiritually mature might start screaming and even go as far as packing her clothes to leave her marital home. All attempts by her husband to explain to her that this is the first time the lady is ever calling him and he doesn't know the reason for her call will fall on deaf ears. He might even forget that he isn't meant to swear as a Christian but goes ahead to swear just to convince her that he has absolutely nothing to do with her any longer. Some thoughtful husbands might even ask their wives to pick the call and talk to the other lady. All of the above would fall on deaf ears just because the enemy wants married couples to be in constant disunity so that he can be free to cause havoc in their homes at will.

Truly, the African adage that says, "He who the gods wants to destroy, they first of all make mad" is so true.

Have you ever quarrelled with your spouse that at the end of it all, you ask yourself if it was really worth it? The sad thing is that most of the time, the havoc has already been done and it is too late to undo things. This doesn't imply that every issue is orchestrated by the devil. I am only saying something the spiritually mature will be able to discern and understand properly. Some issues are just subtle ways by the enemy to gain access to your marriage and home.

I have trained myself over the years to be spiritually sensitive and mature to know what deserves an angry reaction and what needs me to quickly switch to the spirit realm to wage spiritual warfare against demonic intruders into my home. As a wife, you discover that you and your husband have just had a nice time (either you both just finished having a good session of love making or enjoyed being together, planning the future while laughing heartily in between), you then decide to ask him what he wants to eat for dinner and instead of answering that simple question, he flares up and starts saying some hurtful and irrelevant things. You should be sensitive enough to sense that something isn't just right especially if he isn't the type that acts in such a manner.

You have two options here, either to start praying in your spirit mind or give it back to him 'hot' as they usually say. The choice is yours to make and the outcome, yours to deal with. Talking about praying in your spirit mind, this isn't about screaming and insulting your husband in the process of sounding spiritual or religious. Shouting and saying things like, "I dreamt about this last night. The devil that destroyed your parents' marriage won't see mine. No wonder your father could not keep a woman. The way you are acting is demonic. You keep allowing the devil to use you." These words are actually uncalled for.

Yes, I agree with you that some or all of these sentences might be true but as a wise wife, you do not want to add fuel to a burning fire; do you? I guess not. There have been times when my husband suddenly acts in a way that surprises me or we start arguing suddenly. I immediately pray in my spirit against disunity and in no time, he comes back to his loving and caring nature.

The same also applies to the men; do not see every action of your wife as an intention to challenge your authority. While that might be her true intention sometimes, other times, it might be an attempt of the devil to gain access into your home using the weak point of your wife. You cannot afford to be spiritually careless or think your wife is the only one that has to be spiritually alert and sensitive. Dear husbands, you need to be more spiritually alert. Remember, God expects you to be the head of your home; not only the head in matters that favour you but the head in spiritual matters too.

Having established the fact that there is indeed power in unity, I perceive you're wondering how to achieve unity in marriage. I shall discuss some ways that can help in achieving unity in marriage. Also bear in mind that this is not an exhaustive list.

Be Determined to Be United

Nothing is ever done or achieved without a determination to do it. It is sometimes easy to be united sexually, financially and otherwise but spiritual unity is not so easy. This is because it is the most important type of unity in marriage, especially for Christians and the devil knows the power available to a couple that is united spiritually and will do everything to stop it. One thing that can help in your determination to be united is dwelling on the benefits. If a couple sees no need in being spiritually united, they won't work towards achieving it. In summary, make a decision to be spiritually united with one another and that will make the process towards achieving it easier.

Forgive Quickly

It is such an irony that we find it hard to forgive the person we have been joined together to. I also find it quite amusing that some married couples are quick to forgive others but find it difficult to forgive each other. The same man who preaches to his wife and tells her to tolerant their neighbours, his family members and others does not tolerant his wife. The wife who is ready to forgive her friends over and over again is not ready to forgive her husband. Some husbands even torture their wives emotionally; they refuse to eat her food and sleep in the same room. They avoid speaking to her. The worst is refusing to pray together as a family because of grudges that they have refused to let go of.

Remember that while growing up and even now, we still get offended by the action of our siblings, yet, we forgive over and over again. You might argue and say that blood is thicker than water but that assumption makes me laugh. Is your husband or wife water? They are also your family (family of procreation). I once heard a story of a woman who lost her husband to the cold hands of death because of her unwillingness to forgive him. He was gasping for air at night and kept taping her but she refused to turn to find out the reason for the constant tapping. After a while, she noticed he stopped disturbing her. Then, she turned and discovered that he wasn't breathing again.

I've been married for a good number of years and I know that what I am saying is not so easy, especially for those who grew up in a hostile environment and love to hold on to offences. Some people take pride in being extremely tough and do not forgive easily. What is there to be proud about? Do they give gold medals for that or am I missing something? I have also heard some ladies say, "If you are too soft on men, they will take you for a fool." Trust me when I say that is hasty generalization. If you got married to a man that fears God, continually pray for the fear of God to keep and envelop him. That would keep him from constantly misbehaving, not your constant nagging or refusal to forgive. I have seen a husband of a very tough wife misbehave in such a way that the woman developed health issues. The Bible is right in 1 Samuel 2:9b, "For by strength shall no man prevail."

Know What You Are Against

You might not love a particular thing but when you know the alternative, you will have no choice but to embrace it. I grew up not liking unripe plantain but when I had a health challenge and unripe plantain among other meals that weren't my favourite were recommended for me, I had no choice but to stick to them. In fact, I started loving it and still do even after I was certified fit by my doctor. You might have grown up with the idea of being cool with disunity but this cannot work in a marriage where you expect the Holy Spirit to dwell in. Know that you are against principalities and powers that might want to fight your marriage. Imagine the woman that lost her husband in the story I shared above just because she refused to let go. If they had children, what would she tell them? Daddy was dying and begging for my help but I ignored him because we weren't talking? What about the man's parents and siblings; will they ever forgive her? Fine, she might decide to keep the truth to herself but will she be able to outgrow the feeling of guilt? The story was shared anonymously and we can not know the outcome or the reaction of those related to the man.

Knowing you are against demonic forces that would be happy to see you both split should keep you both spiritually alert. It is easy to receive warning signals about an impending danger when you are united. That's because you are both spiritually tuned up to God. Do not blame God that He didn't give you a warning signal. He does but sometimes, we are so busy with malice and strife such that we cannot hear Him when He speaks. I sincerely pray that God opens our eyes to see what we are against. This is not to scare anybody but to portray the true picture of the way spiritual things are. The Bible states that one will chase one thousand and two will chase ten thousand. If you notice the calculation, it didn't say that two shall chase two thousand. Isn't it logical that if one shall chase one thousand, two should chase two thousand? This isn't a mistake. God expects a lot from Christian couples because He knows what they will be against and they need to be together in unity to achieve it.

Have A Functional Family Altar

Altars are symbolic. All through scriptures, you will see that altars were erected. However, beyond having a family altar, it should be functional. A song writer once said, "Jesus, we need you much more than we know you" and I totally agree with the lyrics. If we don't allow our anger hinder us from surfing the Internet, going about our normal activities and relating with outsiders, why then should we allow it prevent us from communicating with our creator? The enemy knows that most couples are aware that it is wrong to pray while still holding a grudge against themselves and so he does all he can to keep them in a state of perpetual grudge against themselves.

There is something we practice in our home; at the beginning of every new month, birth anniversary and marriage anniversary, we pray for each other. You can try that. You cannot hate someone you genuinely pray for. Have days set aside for fasting, either once a week, once a month or as you both are led to. Study the word of God together and let each one share his/her views. It is the spiritual atmosphere you set in your home that your child/children will come to meet. Apart from this helping you both to be united spiritually, it can speak for your family in times of trouble.

Love Birds Exercise 2.

• Did my personal story, THE EXPERIENCE THAT NEARLY TOOK MY LIFE, teach you anything on the power of unity in marriage?

• Do you find it difficult to forgive your spouse? If yes, consciously learn to let go of offences.

• When last did you pray and study the Bible together as a couple?

• As the man, you're the spiritual head of your home. Draw out a roster for your family devotion. For instance, who would take the praise session, prayer session, and the sermon?

• Make up your mind to never stay angry with your spouse.

• If you're single, be sure you agree with your would-be spouse on how to make your family altar burn for Christ.

CHAPTER THREE

DEALING WITH EXTERNAL FORCES

The term 'external forces' is not used in a bad light. It is rather used to represent third party in a marriage. It is important to note that this is not a problem in itself. It only becomes an issue when they are trying to influence the marriage negatively.

Therefore, shall a man leave his father and mother and shall cleave unto his wife; and they shall be one flesh."
Genesis 2:24

Sadly, some couples are not yet ready to leave. Some claim they have left but their actions show that they haven't, while others have actually left but are so confused on how to deal with external forces. Does getting married automatically make everyone your enemy? No, it doesn't but you need wisdom to deal with some people especially those who aren't ready to know that a lot of things or at least a few things will definitely change and change is constant and good. We don't have to always see change in a negative light.

When my elder brother got married, I cried. I knew he was married to a homely, beautiful and nice lady but I was mature enough to know that some things will have to change. We are the only two siblings that attended the same nursery school, primary school, secondary school and university. We left the country together for further studies and still attended the same university over there. Thankfully, his marriage didn't change that relationship but I was smart enough to adjust. Most times, he would visit me and be in a hurry to leave because of his wife; other times, he would decline my offer for dinner knowing that his wife would have prepared dinner at home and is waiting for him to get back home so that they can eat together.

Some in-laws are not willing to adjust to the fact that mummy's once little boy is now married and a grown man. They are not willing to admit that daddy's once little girl is now somebody's wife and a grown woman. They should know that they can't just walk into your matrimonial room without knocking and waiting to get a positive response from you except your spouse is cool with it or not around. Even when your siblings come visiting, especially younger siblings, they should be at their best behaviour. Most in-laws do not do it purposely or with the intention of offending their children's spouse. They honestly do not know that it isn't the right thing to do.

Our pastor once shared his experience during his sermon on a particular Sunday that was dedicated to marriage. He said he grew up to be his mother's favourite son and after he got married, whenever his mother visited him, he noticed that his mother would not knock before entering their room. Most times, she would join him and his wife on the bed talking for long with no intention of leaving any time soon. The most annoying time was that she fondly interrupted them each time they wanted to have a 'great time' together. She would join them in the room and still refuse to go. It went on that way until his wife was terribly upset about it one day. Although she didn't say a word, he could sense it. Moreover, he had spent enough time with her to know when she is angry. He had to have a discussion with his mother. Initially, it took her time to adjust but overtime, she did.

Another husband might not have handled it well. He would have said, "After all, my wife hasn't complained verbally." You don't have to wait for her to do that. You should be able to read her countenance in some situations. You should also know that she might be careful about airing her feelings, especially if you both just got married before you accuse her of wanting to create enmity between you and your mother.

Another set of husbands might be so angry that their wives are even complaining about their mothers always coming into their matrimonial room without knocking. To make it worse, they would twist what their wives are trying to say to suit them and might even ask funny questions like, "Should I abandon my mother just because I am married? If my mother didn't give birth to me, would you have gotten me as a husband?'' and the likes of such irrelevant and unrelated questions.

Dear young married man, get this right. Sometimes, turn the tables. Would you like it if your wife's mother does the same? Ask yourself the exact question you are asking your wife. Would you have gotten her as a wife if her mother didn't give birth to her? Enough of the emotional blackmail. See reasons with what your wife is saying and address the issue rightly and objectively. For the wives, don't condone your parents' ill behaviour towards your husband. What you wouldn't want his parents to do to you, also shield him and prevent your parents from doing that to him.

I grouped external forces after marriage into three major categories and we shall discuss them one after the other for clarity and better understanding.

Family Members

Marriage does not cut you off from loved ones and it doesn't mean that you have to abandon your family members. It only has to be handled with wisdom especially when some family members do not want to understand that things cannot be the same. Like I stated earlier, change must not always be viewed as something wrong. Coincidentally, my husband and I have a very close relationship with our parents and siblings; the bond is so great and strong. He loves, respects and adores his family members just the way I love mine. The good thing is that we both have parents and family members who are mature, loving and above all, spiritually sound. They respect the institute of marriage greatly and so we have never had to choose between our family members and ourselves. We have had our parents and siblings visit us many times but they know their limits.

The issue arises when family members refuse to know their limits. How can your siblings visit you and make the home a living hell for your spouse? I have heard stories of younger siblings of the husband visiting and wanting to do absolutely nothing in the house. They eat and leave their plates unwashed and cannot do the least thing which is tidying up the room they stay in. The most pitiful part is if the wife is a nursing mother or a working class lady. She is sometimes forced to become a glorified house girl in her own matrimony home. She rushes back from work, attends to her baby or children, quickly fixes dinner before her husband returns home, washes the plates her husband's younger siblings used during the day, cleans the house and does other chores.

It is not a beautiful sight at all. The man might notice it but is afraid to talk to his people before they return back with stories of him not being man enough or how the woman is controlling him. Husbands, please protect your wives from your troublesome family members. Wives, please do the same. It might look as if I am just focusing on husbands; this is so because of the power vested in the man. Moreover, some husbands will not hesitate to send the wife's siblings away if they are misbehaving or if he thinks they are but will suddenly develop cold feet when the reverse is the case. You know your siblings and family members better. You should know the one you allow to stay for years in your home and the one that you shouldn't dare allow to visit unless you would be with your wife to protect her from them. There is no need pretending to ourselves. There are some of our siblings that are rude, disrespectful, slothful, lazy and excessively spoilt. There are some family members that you should gladly pay the house rent for them to live alone than allow them spend one day in your home.

How Do I Handle Some Family Members?

— Educate them

Let them know that things have changed. If you had some family members living with you before you got married and you still want them to continue living with you and your wife (of course, after consulting her), it is important to have a discussion with them. Personally, I do not support people staying with a young couple that just got married. They should have some time alone to bond and get to know themselves better. Even if they have dated for donkey years, marriage is a different ball game. That being said, I know that there are some circumstances beyond one's control that might lead to having family members stay with you immediately after marriage. Lovingly tell them that you are still there for them but they need to understand that things might change a little and if they love you, they shouldn't allow you be in a situation where you have to choose between them and your spouse. Present your spouse to them in a loving and respectful way. Glow with excitement as you talk about your spouse. Tell your younger siblings that you expect them to assist in the house chores. If possible as the man, be the one to assign the duties if it is your siblings that will be living with you and your wife. They are more likely to accept it joyfully if it comes from their direct relation than from your wife.

Engage Their Emotions

You can tell them a story of something you learnt from your parents. Words like, "You know daddy and mummy taught us to be at our best behaviour while away from home. Don't disgrace our family here." If they are your aged parents, remind them tactfully that they also have daughters and won't want her in-laws to maltreat her or make her uncomfortable in her own husband's house. Lovingly plead with them to take your wife as their own child.

Begin with Yourself

We lead by example and marriage is not an exception. You cannot expect your family members to treat your spouse with utmost respect while you do the exact opposite. No! It does not work that way. If you need them to consult your wife or husband before taking major decisions that concern you both, be the first to do it. This can be done in such a tactful manner that you unconsciously send a clear message to them and position their minds to do same.

For example as the man, your younger sister who is staying with you asks what you guys would have for dinner. Instead of saying anything you like when your wife is at home, you can ask her to confirm from your wife if there isn't dinner already. Don't make the mistake of allowing your younger sister run the home and call the shots. This can be allowed if your wife permits it or if she is so busy. Do not ask what the big deal is. It might not be a big deal to you but your wife might start processing it in another light and believe me, it is not a pleasant feeling because most wives like to be in charge of their kitchen.

Let your siblings know that you won't take a major decision without discussing with your spouse first. It gives your spouse a sense of belonging and involvement. Let me address the ladies specifically here as we are sometimes the ones who tend to be emotional and refuse to reason rationally. Assuming your siblings call you to ask if they can come around for holiday, even if you know that your husband will not object to it, tell them you would get back to them after informing your husband or you can even ask them to call him directly. Isn't he now part of the family? Don't act as if you alone can call the shot even if that is what is obtainable in your home.

Do you want your family members to respect your husband as the head of the family? Start respecting him even in his absence. Let them know that he is your earthly king as it is ordained to be. Do you want your family members to value the opinion of your wife? See her as joint heirs with you and respect her in spite of her age. Let it begin with you, her husband. The love my elder brother has for his wife is so contagious that we also love, accept and respect her. I call her 'big sis' and it's so easy to do so because of how he has placed her.

Friends

Friendship is a beautiful thing. It feels good to have people who are not related to you by blood but have a place in your life. There are some friends that aren't close to us. We call them friends when in reality, they are just acquaintance and therefore, letting go of such friendships is so easy but friendship of years that began from childhood can sometimes be difficult to break or do without. Marriage does not require you to cut off from good and meaningful friendships. The emphasis is on 'good' and 'meaningful'. It is true that some friends already understand the institution of marriage and the fact that it can change some things, not necessarily the bond or attachment but the duration of time spent together might have to reduce. It is a good thing that the quality might still be the same.

For instance, a lady who could spend hours after work on Skype or chatting with various friends on all the social media platforms before marriage might have to reduce that except her husband is away on official duties or not home at that time. This is because he might need her in bed and they might have something important to discuss. She might even have her children's meal and laundry to think about.

Mature friends will understand, although others might feel left out or think you are feeling above them. The good news is that they will get to understand once they are married. Most times, people do not understand until they get to the same position and experience what you've experienced. The funny thing is that they might not be able to manage things the way you did or are doing.

I heard of someone who was angry that her friend wasn't visiting her as often as she was visiting before she got married. Her friend tried explaining things to her that she got a new job and got pregnant immediately. The effect of pregnancy plus a change of job and other household chores expected of a married woman was too much on her. At least, she was still trying to create time for their friendship but her explanation fell on deaf ears. Funnily enough, she wasn't upset because she knew her friend wouldn't really understand until she gets married.

A year later, the friend got married. She forgot to keep in touch for the first three weeks. Her friend called her and she started apologizing and explaining that it has been quite overwhelming for her to settle down in a new place and adjust to a new life.

Also, the men that tend to laugh at their married male friends, calling them 'woman wrapper' and 'lover boy' usually do more than that for their spouse when they eventually settle down.

Your wife or husband is not asking you to cut off from your friends. They simply want you to put them first when they need you the most. Your wife cannot be sick and crying in pains while you leave her to hang out with the boys. This is so insensitive of you especially when it is not a do or die affair. Your wife cannot be in the hospital to give birth to your child and you are with your friends in the name of *It is my friend's birthday*. Dear young married man, is it his last birthday? Are you the oxygen of the party that without your presence, the party won't hold? On a second thought, how would your friends know that your wife is in the hospital alone in labour and not drive you away from that party insisting that you must be there with your wife? Some friends will even go the extra mile to be there with you if there is a complication and you need emotional support. Good friends will not attempt to come between you and your wife and if they try to do so, you should be able to say no. It doesn't make you a bad person. Don't let friends put enmity between you and your spouse while they go to sleep after setting your marital home on fire.

There was a young man who had an issue with his wife. His friend was with him and noticed that the wife didn't serve his food properly. He asked her to bring drinking water for them and she delayed a bit. His friend started making him see things differently, telling him that he needed to teach her a lesson, if not, she would keep repeating the same mistake and it might get to a point that she would start talking to him in public. Right there, he acted on the words of his friend and gave his new wife the humiliation of her life. He pushed her to the wall and slapped her. She was so shocked that she couldn't utter a word. She simply left the parlour to their bedroom. His friend cheered him up and called him a real man.

Months later, he accompanied his friend to his house. The wife served them food and as she went to get water, he wanted to show he was in charge. He screamed at her to get water. She screamed back as this was a strange behaviour to her. His friend expected him to beat her up, knowing how he pushed him to do same to his wife but surprisingly, he started apologising to his wife. His friend was so shocked that he couldn't eat the food that was served. He rushed back to his wife and sincerely apologised to her. He learnt that lesson early in his marriage and was the one sharing the story with young couples years later.

Friends can only advise you. It is left for you to accept or reject it. You are in charge of the level at which they influence your marriage. Any friend that loves you and values your peace of mind will not cheer you to do anything that can be detrimental to the success of your marriage. If they don't love you and your marriage, you should love yourself and your marriage. At the end of the day, when the chips are down, some of your friends might be nowhere to be found. Only your spouse would stand solely by you.

'Well-Wishers'

If you are not African, this might not make much sense to you but a lot of Africans can understand and relate with what I am about to say. These well-wishers might not necessarily be our family members or friends. They could be acquaintances who wish the best for us or at least, we think that they do. A lot of people do not mind their business. They leave unsolicited pieces of advice and hurtful remarks. It is left for couples to disregard their remarks or hold unto it. A couple can be okay with themselves managing their present state, while of course, trusting God that things get better. While working towards that, a total stranger from nowhere says a word that if not well managed by the receiver can shake the very foundation of that marriage. A wife can be so happy while washing her husband's clothes and the 'well-wisher' in the form of a neighbour can just make a careless comment, "Why are you still washing clothes with your hand in this era? Don't tell me your husband cannot afford a washing machine. Are you sure he is not keeping another family outside? You know you are yet to give him children." A wife that doesn't understand the tactics of joy killers who sometimes come in the form of 'well-wishers' could get irritated or start crying. Some who cannot wait for the man to come back home would call and pour out their frustration on the young man who is out there trying his best to provide for his family.

In as much as it is important to listen to what people have to say, do not let those who do not matter control your marriage. Even if the things they have to tell you are true, those messages can be passed in a pleasant way without them trying to scorn you indirectly.

I attended a close friend's wedding in 2014 and after that, she left the country for medical check-up because she fell very sick and all the tests run on her showed that nothing was wrong. Thankfully, she is completely healed by God who is the greatest physician. Before then, she felt she was going to die. Sometimes, she even had suicidal thoughts because the pains were unbearable. Doctors already told her that she can't get pregnant in that state and frankly, pregnancy was the last thing on her mind. All she wanted was total healing. During that time, a lot of 'well-wishers' not knowing what she was going through publicly made hurtful and insensitive comments like, "Get pregnant quickly. What are you waiting for? Are you living with your brother?" She went through this for four years.

Do you see why you shouldn't allow well-wishers control your home? They don't even know what you are going through. Here was a woman fighting to live and everyone was praying for her. There were times she called me over the phone and asked that I pray for her. Sometimes, my husband and I would pray for her but I never really knew that it was that bad. I am so happy that as I write this book, she is completely healed and her health fully restored. Learn to ignore side talks that affect your peace because these people might not really understand what you feel.

We have established that the term 'external' isn't used in a bad light. Maintaining a close relationship with family members, friends and well-wishers isn't in itself bad. In fact, we need them in the journey of marriage and that's why I get worried when newlyweds cut off from people that mean well for them or have been an integral part of their lives.

It only becomes an issue when the couple allows them dictate the tone in their marriage to their own detriment. Wisdom is needed when relating with these people to avoid unpleasant stories of excessive control and dictation from them.

Love Birds Exercise 3.

• Are external forces already causing issues in your marriage?

• As a couple, decide now to never act on the opinion of others without taking each other's feelings into consideration?

• Get a sheet of paper and write down areas that you have allowed the influence of external forces.

• What are you putting in place to avoid external influence in your marriage?

• If you're single, discuss and agree with your would-be spouse about what you two would accept in your home and what you would not.

CHAPTER FOUR

KILLERS OF JOY IN MARRIAGE

arriage was originally created by God for companionship, pleasure, procreation, bliss and everything good. The sorrow we see in marriages today is as a result of man's disobedience to the rules of marriage.

Every institution has laid down rules and regulations, including marriage. Isn't it funny that we stick to the rules at our place of work, churches and associations but refuse to stick to the rules for a blissful marriage?

In this chapter, we shall dwell on some killers of joy in marriage. The fact that a couple is still living together does not mean that they are enjoying their marriage.

Infidelity

"Marriage is honourable in all, and the bed undefiled."

Hebrews 13: 4a

Sometimes, I wonder if some couples do not understand the marriage vows they took on the day of their wedding

...with my body, I do honour you.

Why then are you bringing dishonour to your spouse by being unfaithful? Many wives have been mocked and dishonoured by little girls, most of whom are less educated and much younger than them, just because their husband won't keep his penis inside his trousers. The worse is when he makes that delicate organ of his body that should be for only his wife a community penis. Some husbands take it to the extreme by bringing the woman or women into their homes. Nothing kills joy in marriages than this. A lot of wives are depressed, moody, gloomy and even have health issues because of this. A greater percentage wish to take a walk out of their marriages but are just afraid of what the society would say. It is such an irony that the 'one' person whose joy and happiness should be your priority is the one you hurt badly.

I once counselled a young wife whose husband was a chronic cheat. The day I walked into the fixed venue to see her, I almost wept; the only reason I acted strong was because she needed me to be strong for her. She was a shadow of herself and joy had practically left her. I watched her narrate her ordeal and gave the best counsel I knew. In fact, as I got home that day, I couldn't think straight for days. I have heard different stories and handled numerous cases that involve infidelity but this case was so emotional for me, probably because she was young, stressed out and battling with health complications as a result of the issue. I seriously cannot tell but the memory of that appointment still remains fresh in my mind.

I do say that it is easy for a wife to handle external pains but when it is coming directly from the person she has left her family of orientation for, a man that she must have turned down numerous suitors for or sacrificed for; nothing hurts that much. It is not just an issue of sleeping with someone else but an issue of betrayal of trust.

I wish men can understand this better. Do not be the reason your wife cries to bed every night. It can be dangerous. Dear young husband, it is not about blurting, "I cheated only once." No! It is deeper than that. Most affairs leave a woman traumatized for the rest of her life unless God intervenes.

A highly placed woman and a renowned politician shared her story of how her husband cheated on her. Before the incident, she trusted him with her life and believed all he said until she caught him in the very act. It affected her so badly that she confessed to not believing people when they speak. You can imagine how her husband's affair is now affecting the way she relates with others. This hurts more when the marriage is yet to be blessed with children. What if your one-time sex gets the other woman pregnant? You torment your wife more as she would always be on the edge.

Believe me, you don't need the woman who is always on the edge as a wife. Do you know that it is also possible for your wife to have an affair and get pregnant immediately? Oh yes! Some delays are not physical but spiritual; more of an attempt of the devil to cause a couple to have children outside their marriage. Do not give the devil a space in your home.

What about the medical implications? So many men have brought incurable diseases home to their wives because they refused to zip up and have self-control. The spiritual implication is even more dangerous. If you are a strong Christian, you will agree that sex isn't just sex. It is much more than inserting your penis in a vagina and ejaculating. Little wonder, spirits can be transferred during sexual intercourse and sex can be used by demonic kingdoms to enslave people who are ignorant of this fact.

Months ago, a story was shared on Instagram about a man who picked up a lady on his way back from work. While he was happy that the lady agreed to keep him company that night, he didn't know she was far from being an ordinary lady. According to him, he had a great time, paid her off and she left the next day but since she left, it was from one strange and frightful experience to another. He kept seeing himself having sex with her every night and he would wake up wet. His business started going down. In fact, nothing was working anymore. That was when he decided to put out his story online for people to advise him on what to do. A lot of people told him he needs deliverance. I was quite shocked that he waited to be told it was a spiritual case. From all the signs, he should have known that the strange happenings around him weren't mere coincidence.

I didn't follow up on the story and I don't know how it ended. It's not about being scared of your wife or not wanting to look like the odd or 'holier than thou' one among your clique. If all your close friends do is disrespect their marriage vows by constantly cheating on their wives, you need to change your friends. It's bad if they are proud about it and joyfully tell you about their escapades with different ladies other than their wives. They tell you of wild and crazy things they do with these ladies in bed and you are tempted to try their lifestyle or you constantly get 'hard' just by listening to them. If you are not careful, they would arrange a new lady for you soon. Our standard is the Bible.

"Be not deceived, evil communications corrupt good manners."

1 Corinthians 15:33

They only tell you the so-called fun part, not the evil entering their lives as a result of this. The truth is that most of them must have noticed it but are helpless and do not know how to put an end to it as most of those ladies would have used charms to tie them and keep them perpetually in bondage. Most of them have started having dreams and seeing themselves in water-like environments. They know they are already possessed by some kind of strange powers. Some hear voices speaking to them and others can no longer maintain an erection while with their wives but do nothing special to last for hours when they are together with these strange ladies.

Many have become a shadow of themselves and they know life is leaving them gradually. They might be envious of you secretly and want to drag you down with them. You need to go for deliverance services to see and hear about the demonic entanglements some men have gotten themselves into for not being faithful to their wives.

Dear young married man, I write to you with love in my heart. Be satisfied with your wife alone. Remember the Bible admonishes in Proverbs 5:19 *"Let her be as the loving hind and pleasant roe, let her breasts satisfy thee at all times; and be thou ravished always with her love."*

If you are not afraid of contacting deadly diseases, your wife's constant nagging, your focus drifted, spending unnecessarily as you now have to maintain two or more ladies depending on the level of your cheating; be at least afraid of being a prey to the devil, thereby exposing your life and family to demonic attack and opening the door to strange experiences.

To The Wives

Infidelity in marriage is not only restricted to the male folks. I am fully aware of the fact that some married women cheat as well. The only exception is that they are more discreet about it. I guess it is because of the way society frowns at it. It is surprising to hear really harsh and strong words used when a woman is unfaithful. A man cheats and people might say, "He is a man. It's their nature. What do you expect of a typical Africa man?" Well, I see the last sentence as an insult to the set of African men who are striving daily to remain faithful to their marital vows.

Let a woman cheat on her husband, even if it is the first time, and she would be tagged a prostitute and loose breed. She might even lose her marriage as a result of that. I am not here to talk about how wrong this is. That is the marginalization and the different judgement meted out on a woman who is caught being unfaithful to her husband. I guess this is so because a higher moral standard is expected from women. This is not in any way excluding the men from upholding such high moral standards.

Wives, you need to cut away from all temptations. It might not come in the form of temptation but you need to be sensitive. Guard your heart and emotions. Do whatever it takes to guard your heart. We are more likely to fall for someone who is always there for us and listens to us; whereas some of our husbands might be too busy to listen to us. For women, it usually starts as an emotional affair. I know most women do not plan sleeping with those they have slept with but things just suddenly got out of control. You find yourself falling for him, meanwhile you originally saw him as your elder brother. Let this sink in you, he is not your elder brother. He might lead you on tactfully because he claims to be in love with you.

I had to take a tough decision which was to avoid counselling men alone physically. If you need physical consultation, it's either you come along with your partner or I come with my beloved husband. It might not go down well with some people but I have to keep the interest of my marriage first after an experience I had.

A very respectful young man booked for a physical consultation. We had connected well online and I thought he was coming with his wife to be. I got there and noticed he was alone. That wasn't an issue because it was an open place and other people were present. However, I noticed he kept staring lustfully at me. I was yet to recover from that awful stare when he said, "I wish I could get your husband out of the way and have you." I immediately covered myself with the blood of Jesus and told him that such joke was too expensive and will not be tolerated by me. I wasn't comfortable any longer and I requested to leave. No doubt, he apologised but I learnt a lesson. Some men will pretend to be in trouble and want only you to save them. Most times, it is a trap. I got back home and narrated the ordeal to my husband and we both laughed about it. Later that day, I wondered what would have happened if we were in an enclosed place. As a married person, you need to be careful.

I once heard a true life story of a married woman. Her husband works on shore and was away for official duties. She was alone with her two children in their beautiful home. One discussion with her ex who is also married led to another and she invited him over. I guess they could not control their emotions and they ended up having sex; not just sex but unprotected sex. I know you are probably wondering if protected sex is less of a sin. No! it isn't. Protected sex is still a sin but unprotected sex just shows how carried away they were and they threw caution away. It was more shocking because they were both married with children and should have been more careful but then, maybe the lady insisted and the man refused. Who knows? When some men are hard down there, nothing else matters to them.

Now back to the story; unknown to her, she took in from that sexual act. You know when the devil wants to disgrace you, he makes sure an indelible mark is left with your first indulgence into sin. Her case was pathetic but she didn't know. Her husband got back home two days later and she had sex with him as well. When she discovered she was pregnant, she thought it was for her husband. She had a smooth pregnancy and delivery but things went tough as soon as she gave birth. The baby fell sick and needed blood transfusion. Her blood group and that of her husband didn't match with their baby's. The doctor immediately knew that something wasn't just right. He decided to run a DNA test and it was discovered that the baby wasn't for the man.

The man was confused and angry at the same time. Her parents got invited and everyone pleaded with her to say something. That was when she opened up and told the truth. Her parents broke into tears begging the man to kindly let go of his anger and disappointment and forgive her. They even promised to take care of the last child who isn't his but their plea fell on deaf ears. The sad thing was that he said he was going to take full custody of his two children. She had to leave that day with the child of her affair and her parents. Her ex who is married told her that she can't ruin his home and happy marriage. He only promised to send money for the upkeep of the child. I felt really bad about it.

As a married woman, you have to be extremely careful. Don't expose yourself to situations that can lead to adultery. Turn down all advances from other men for the sake of God and your marriage.

Handling Delay Badly

A whole chapter shall be dedicated to this; so we shall just talk about it briefly here. Actually, no one likes delay. Even the Bible says in Proverbs 13:12a that hope deferred makes the heart sick. However, there are some things we do not have control over. The only option is to do our part and leave the rest in God's hands. When a couple is experiencing delay in any area of their life, it is usually a very trying time especially when they never saw it coming or cannot understand the reason for the delay. If this is not well handled, it is capable of killing the joy in their marriage.

Allowing Family Intrusion

A young lady walked out of her marriage because her husband was practically controlled by his mother. His mother was the one making the final decisions at home. It would have been better if her son was not supporting his mother but her husband saw nothing wrong with his mother always being the one to call the shots. From the kind of apartment to rent to where they should buy properties to even the tiniest details of their lives.

Dear couples, in as much as we have our family members who do not automatically become unrelated to us because we are married, we still need wisdom on how we allow them intrude in our new home. Don't let someone set your house on fire and go to his/her own house for a sound sleep. I know some sisters-in-law who would not allow their brother's wife enjoy her home. They're always wanting to be in control but they can't stand it when they eventually get married and their husband's sisters do the same to them.
As a couple, you must decide that you won't let family intrusion destroy the joy in your marriage. Your siblings

should know that there are some issues they can discuss with you alone, not your husband or wife. You are their sibling and so you can understand some things and won't misinterpret it or their intentions.

Communicate individually to your families and let them know their limits in your home. If your sister insults your wife once and you keep quiet about it, be rest assured that it will happen next time because your silence means you tolerate it even if you might have kept calm to avoid issues. You need to let your sister know you won't tolerant it next time, even if you have to do that in the absence of your wife especially if she is your elder sister or your wife's senior.

The home is a place everyone should feel free. Don't let your spouse dislike coming home because she is trying to avoid issues from your family. Although it is quite difficult to completely rule out family intrusion from a typical marriage but at least, you can minimize it.

My spiritual father, Bishop David Oyedepo, says this always, "What you don't want, you don't watch. "This doesn't just apply to spiritual matters but to every sphere of your life you choose to apply it to. In this case, your marital life. Don't sit down and allow them maltreat your wife. She committed no crime by accepting to marry you and become a member of your family. Wives, don't allow them rule over your husband. He is your earthly king, not an errand boy.

Technology

As good as technology is, if not well handled, it can kill joy in marriages. Gone are the days when couples wake up and the first thing they do is pray together or have an intimate discussion or just bond together talking and sharing great stories. These days, some couples reach for their phones immediately they get out from bed. They can spend as much as three hours or more surfing the net and the minute their spouse wants to discuss anything with them, they suddenly remember they would soon be late for work. So they quickly suggest that it will be better to talk after work. Without even getting an answer, they jump off while their spouse have so much inside of them begging for expression and someone to listen to them pour out their deepest fears, dreams or aspirations. Sadly, the only time some couples have time for each other is when they want to have sex. The other partner might have noticed this ugly trend and is already irritated. Such a person no longer gives in his/her best to this pleasurable act in marriage.

The cycle continues once the sex is over. One or both partners get back to the phone laughing with people who do not really matter and even if they do matter, that can be done later. How about discussing the sex you both just had? How about scoring each other and laughing heartily like little children without a care in the world? Fine, if you do not believe in talking about sex; what about cuddling each other and enjoying each other's arms in silence? Most people have let technology rob them of the joy of so many interesting things that marriage has to offer. These days, some of them do not care if their partners are talking to them or not. They have enough friends to talk to online, after all, Facebook allows a maximum of 5,000 friends.

Now, I understand the sense in a book I read some years ago. The author said if he has his way, he would want new couples to live without technology for one year. That sounds too long and awkward but knowing what I know today, I totally understand the angle he was coming from. I say this with no iota of false thinking; if you take the phones of some couples for days, they would have to start knowing each other afresh. Technology is good but you should own it, not the other way round. Your husband might be struggling at his place of work to get the attention of his boss. Should he struggle at home to get his wife's attention as well? Some wives do not mind laughing at some posts online or chatting with friends when their husbands want them to serve their food. You should have set the table if you got home earlier than him and if you didn't, you should do it as soon as he gets home and if that still didn't occur to you, at least do it as he is asking you to do it. This might not go down well for some feminist but this is for the women that believe they should take care of their husbands, especially when they can.

I know that we are all humans and we can get carried away with some conversations but that's when maturity and priority comes in. Is the chat more important than giving my husband his food? If it is, can I appeal to him in a kind and tactful manner to please hold on while I quickly round off? Or do I act as if he should automatically understand what I am doing online?

I was a guest speaker at an online event which was to last for about an hour but it ended up lasting for close to three hours. I had already informed my husband about it because I knew he was going to wait for me to finish up before we retire to bed. When I noticed I was spending longer time than I prepared his mind for, I ran to him in the parlour, gave him a peck on his cheeks while telling him, "Baby, I will soon be done." It went on that way until I finally concluded the session. If you must choose what you are doing online at the moment your spouse needs you over your spouse, respectfully explain to them and plead for their understanding.

How about you, the husband? Do you listen to your wife or let technology steal you away from her every time? It is either you are at work, hanging out with the boys, away on official meetings, chatting online or constantly surfing the Internet. Some men think women must always talk even if they have nothing to say; so they feel listening to her is a complete waste of time but believe me when I say it isn't. Most women who ended up having an affair outside didn't do it because they really wanted. They somehow saw that man as a listening fellow. The man might have been the type who listens to all she had to say, sense and nonsense inclusive, and in no time, they got carried away and let down their guard. Most men cannot remember the last complain their wives made or the last important thing she said. I am not supporting extra-marital affairs. I can never do that. Wives, please take note. The point here is that men should learn to listen to their wives and satisfy their emotional needs.

Use of Hurtful Words

Don't speak before thinking. That's why marriage is only for mature adults. If you have something to say, try as much as you can to say it in a respectful manner. I understand that at times, we might be so angry that we say whatever we want to say. Others even think that not saying hurtful or mean words means you are afraid of the other person. They often claim openly that they're not afraid of anyone and that they can say things the way it is. In marriage, you need to watch the words you say if you are the type that has no control over your words when angry. It is better to keep quiet than to say words that you will forever regret.

A lady suddenly broke into tears as she remembered all the hurtful words her husband had been using on her. The most surprising part was that some of these words were used on her years ago but she could still remember them vividly. The worse is involving your spouse's parents in any misunderstanding and using nasty and disrespectful words on them. Marriage is only for the mature. Why would you involve your spouse's parents in your misunderstanding? It is simple; you want them to be deeply hurt when you know they hold their parents in high esteem. Instead of looking for a way to settle the issue amicably and early enough, you escalate it by hurting not only your spouse's feelings but insulting their parents too. Most times, you know that what you are about to say doesn't make sense or isn't true but because you are bent on hurting the other person, you spill out hurtful comments.

For example, you know your wife's mother separated from her husband because of his abusive nature that nearly sent her to an early grave and she had to be admitted to a mental home to be stabilized but because you are angry with your wife, you go ahead to tell her that she is just behaving like her mother or you say, "No wonder your father almost beat your mother to death. I think you people cannot stay in a man's house." It is wisdom to keep shut when angry. In reality, the man might even be living alone as all attempt to remarry has failed due to his abusive nature which has also chased other women away. Does it mean every lady also left him because they couldn't stay in a man's house? You know the truth but you want to use hurtful words to get back at your wife. It might take your wife time to forgive you especially if she told you the history of her parents' failed marital life out of trust. On a second thought, she might actually forgive you but not forget how you spilled those words shamelessly. She might forgive you and forget but she will never open up to tell you her family's secrets since it is obvious that things you are told out of trust will be used against her in another heated argument.

Wives, also listen. Most of us do not think before talking. Do you think seasoning your words with salt is a weakness and the man will take you for granted?

"Let your speech be always with grace, seasoned with salt, that ye may know how to answer every man."

Colossians 4:6

Even when your husband says something very hurtful, you have a choice to ignore it or give it back to him. Pay attention to this true life story. A man got married to a lady who came from a family of perpetual divorce. Most of her siblings had left their spouses due to one unresolved issue or the other. She knew God and resolved within herself to make her own marriage work. One day, she did something that offended her husband and he couldn't control himself in public as he said something really hurtful. I can't remember the exact words but it was something about her trying to go the same way of her siblings who weren't able to last in a man's house. As God will have it, she sensed the argument could escalate if she didn't handle it well. With tears in her eyes, she asked, "Did you have to bring my siblings into this? If we don't know how to love and submit to a man, why not teach me or aren't you the head of our home and my teacher?" The man that was narrating the story to his friends said he cried, took her inside their room and apologised to her. That was the end of him ever bringing her family into any issue they had.

What if she reacted? What if she also brought in his own family? After all, we all have some things in our family that we aren't proud of. Your guess is as good as right.

Back to the wives; maybe your husband's father couldn't leave anything behind before he died. He might have been a womanizer and spent all his life savings on women. His wife already knew about this deadly lifestyle of her husband but decided to stay. We all know how it was in those days. They were taught to endure a lot of things. Your husband must have told you that with regret in his voice, knowing the kind of money and opportunities their late father was exposed to at a very young age but squandered everything on the laps of women. You consoled him and encouraged him to forgive his late father but because you are suspecting a lady that called him who might not have anything to do with him, you then use what he told you about his late father to insult him. "Good for nothing husband. Who is calling you? I don't blame you. Your father's blood runs in you or aren't you the son of your father? If you like, repeat the mistake of your father. Show me one property in this world that your father left behind. Of course, none. Why don't we start from your village? He couldn't even erect a mud house in your village. You really had a useless father."

Do you know that those words can pierce through any man's heart no matter how huge he is? It takes a lot of self-control not to fight back or try to teach one a lesson.

Watch the words you use on each other. They are capable of destroying the joy in your marriage. If you have to see a therapist, please do. If you have to learn how to manage anger, please do. If you need to keep quiet when angry, please do. Whatever you think can help you stay calm and think carefully before spilling out words, please do them.

Over-familiarity

This is common between couples that dated for so long or cohabited before marriage. There is this tendency of getting over-familiar with each other. This in itself isn't bad but it becomes an issue when it leads to disrespect which can eventually kill joy in marriage. Your husband is trying to air his opinion on an issue being discussed but you keep shutting him up with insensitive and insulting comments such as "What do you know? When did you become a commenter? Please keep quiet and let intelligent people talk." The most annoying part is you might go out and get the exact piece of advice that you called rubbish because it came from your husband. This might be the reason some husbands keep quiet at home but are the life of the party outside their homes. They rarely give you an answer when you ask for their opinion. What is the need when you will eventually do what you feel like doing? You do not even apply tact in refusing the idea he gives you. You might have asked, "Baby, what do you think about starting an importation business?" and he is trying to tell you that it is a good idea but you need to do a comprehensive market survey for the needs of people before importing goods so you do not have to import goods that people do not really need and struggle to sell. That's a good point if you ask me. He is not discouraging you from starting an importation business; he only advised you to do proper research. Out of over-familiarity, some wives have no regard for their husbands. Most of them might begin a sarcastic laugh saying, "Oga research, I hear you. I only want to import goods. I didn't say I want to go back to school again." To avoid trouble, the man might keep quiet and let her do what she wants to do. She goes ahead and gets the goods without proper research of what people need. Four months later, she still hasn't been able to sell a single product. Frustrated, she complains to the same husband whose wise counsel she refused to heed to. Of course, he would just smile and watch her pour out her frustration while he blocks his mind to avoid being contaminated with her bad energy. If he gave her the money for that business, there might be serious issues and that can lead to temporary disagreement. While she is complaining of no sales, he is so bitter and angry with her for not listening to his advice. Learn not to take your spouse for granted.

What about the issue of serving food properly for your husband? It is such a pity that some wives only bring out the best plates and cutleries when there is an occasion because they want to impress their guests and give them the best dining experience but serve their husbands food anyhow with plastic plates, rubber spoon and the like. Meanwhile in reality, you should strive to treat your husband like a king. It isn't wrong if you keep a set of plates and cutleries for him alone. We do not mind giving the best of meals to visitors. In some homes, the moment you see the wife going for fruit and beverage shopping, it's obvious she's expecting a visitor at home. The moment you see her browsing the Internet and looking for different delicacies and how to cook them, it means someone is about to visit them. It is such an irony that the one person that should come first now comes last after everybody. What about the set of wives that bow down to serve everyone apart from their husbands? Don't get me wrong; I do not believe in bowing down to serve people food as that isn't my culture. I wasn't brought up that way. Moreover, my husband doesn't mind but what I am against is doing that for every guest and everyone apart from your husband.

Some men have gotten so familiar with their wives that they do not take her advice seriously. I won't forget an experience of a well-known politician. He was to go for a function and his wife called him and told him the dream she had. In that dream, he was humiliated. He quickly knew that what could cause him such humiliation was if he does not deliver his speech excellently. Then, he decided to start practicing daily and put in more effort. He got called up to deliver his speech the day he wasn't originally scheduled to do so. He did excellently such that his senior colleagues kept congratulating him days after the event. That was when he understood that his wife's dream was to make him prepare adequately and that saved him from shame. What if he ignored his wife's dream? What if he had gotten so familiar with her that he felt her words were meaningless? As I type this, I remember the story of a man who lost his life in a ghastly motor accident. We were told his wife had a terrible dream about him and warned him not to travel for that period. He overlooked it and travelled but never returned. Do you know the kind of grief he brought to his wife? While it is very true that some things beyond our control can happen, it is even truer that if spouses do not take each other for granted as a result of over-familiarity, some things can be avoided. The women are more align to sense things spiritually. Instead of just waving aside the dreams she has or her feelings, how about praying together and nullifying the bad dream?

The danger of over-familiarity is that we tend to care less about how the other person really feels. We are all created to be loved and accepted; our views and everything that makes us unique.

Don't get too familiar with your spouse in such a way that it affects your relationship with each other negatively. No doubt, many things will change after marriage but let's try to still respect and love each other as couples who know the true meaning of marriage and have chosen to value themselves in spite of the years they have spent together and the many more years they will still spend together.

Bringing Up the Past Repeatedly

Your spouse might have wronged you in the past but bringing it up repeatedly can be frustrating for them and this is capable of killing the joy in your marriage. If they have genuinely apologised and you have decided to forgive them, please find a way to totally avoid bringing it up. They might have done things that you still shiver at the thought of but know that they might not also be proud of those things they have done.

For instance, your husband cheated on you with his secretary at work. I know that infidelity is one of the biggest killers of joy in marriages. You didn't catch him red-handed but he confessed to you because the guilt was killing him. He was so affected by this that he had to take out some days for a spiritual retreat. I know that doesn't make it less hurtful. He wept while asking for your pardon and you forgave him but you keep bringing it up at the slightest provocation. You don't even allow him feel free again at home. If he is trying to be happy, you suddenly ask why he should be happy. If he is calm and lost in thoughts, you ask if he is thinking of the secretary. If he comes back late from work, you ask if he was with the secretary. You just make her part of your daily life and bring her up anytime you and your husband have something to discuss. The worse is having an anniversary for it. Maybe he told you he cheated on you on 15th November, 2015. So every 15[th]November, you get moody and start crying. He is confused that he probes further to find out what the issue is and you tell him it's the anniversary of his unfaithfulness. This might sound funny but some women can do this.

Men are not left out of this. The fact that your wife told you of her past life doesn't mean you should always rub it on her face. She might have done some things in the past that she isn't proud of; maybe she had an abortion or dated a married man and she deemed it fit to tell you. It is not right to keep bringing it up every time you two have a misunderstanding. That's the reason some ladies keep shut about their life and act like saints. There was a young lady who got married. Before then, she told her husband-to-be that she had an abortion in the past. Six months into the marriage, she was yet to conceive. Her husband told her bluntly that it was as a result of the abortion she had in the past. She was so hurt and immediately decided to see a gynaecologist who ran comprehensive tests but couldn't find anything wrong with her. He requested that she brings her husband. He refused at first, telling her that he already has a child from a woman in his past and he cannot be the one with the issue. His wife had no choice but to stop seeing any gynaecologist as the one she saw couldn't find anything wrong with her and they always insisted she brings her husband. When he saw she wasn't set to go for any other medical appointment without him, he reluctantly decided to go with her. It came as a shock when the test conducted on him showed that he had no active sperm cell. That incident almost broke their marriage. His lack of active sperm cell wasn't his wife's main reason for being mad. She was angry that he kept bringing up her past mistake whereas the root cause of her delayed conception was from him, not her.

Comparison

This is another killer of joy in marriages. No one loves to be compared unfavourably with others. Many couples do this to spark up jealousy in their spouse's heart but this is wrong in every way. Telling your wife that you wish she was like another woman or comparing your husband to another man who you think treats his wife better is an error. Young couples, you can effectively pass your message across without comparison. If you see something you admire in a couple, you can lovingly tell your partner.

For example, you and your wife paid another couple a visit and you enjoyed the Afang soup you were served. You can lovingly tell your wife something like this, "Baby, I do enjoy the Afang soup you have been cooking but I also liked the way Mrs. A's Afang soup tasted. It was so spicy." Do you know that your wife will not mind going to learn how to cook spicy Afang soup from Mrs. A? However, if you pass the message in a rude manner and make it worse by saying something that sounds like this, "If they keep Mrs. A's Afang soup and yours, hers will beat yours. Her husband is really enjoying. I wish you were like her" and the likes of such immature comments, your wife might react badly. Depending on her temperament, it might turn into a heated argument that you will not be able to contain. She might even start having contempt for you secretly or nursing envy for Mrs. A. She might start seeing her as a rival and decline openly the next time you ask her to accompany you to another friend's house.

If you want to be truthful to yourself, there might be other great meals that your wife can cook very well that Mrs. A cannot cook. Afang soup is just one type of food out of thousands. On the other hand, Mrs. A's husband might be giving her good money to cook whereas your wife is managing the little money you usually give her.

Dear young wives, the fact that your friend's husband helps her in the kitchen always doesn't mean your husband is not trying if he doesn't do same. Your friend's husband might have a job that gives him time to do that comfortably while yours might have to work from 06:00am to 09:00pm including Saturdays. Most times, we compare without thinking.

I spent the Christmas of 2018 alone because my husband was out of town on official duties. Yet, most of my married friends spent theirs with their husbands around. It would be lack of wisdom on my part if I compare him to other men who spent theirs with their wives. Their jobs are not the same with my husband's job. However, I can respectfully tell him that I felt lonely spending the Christmas alone without bringing in anyone's husband into the picture.

Also, the people you compare yourselves with might secretly wish to be like you, even if you think they have all you desire. Comparison is not the way forward. You can pick what you like in other people's marriages and duplicate in yours. The other couple you are comparing your young marriage to might have done worse when they got married newly but with constant zeal to apply godly knowledge and biblical marriage success principles, they are where they are today; a place you admire. I have an elderly couple that I admire a lot and look up to; all I did was to get close to the wife and ever since then, I've been learning and applying the knowledge to my marriage. This is a better way to enjoy your marriage without comparison.

Too Much Unrealistic Expectations

It's certain that marriage makes life better for us and as such, we have some things we expect from our spouse and some duties we owe them as well. Notwithstanding, too many unrealistic expectations can ruin the joy in marriages.

Do you know that our spouse might be suffering from severe depression unknown to us? We expect them to make us happy all the time but it is impossible for them to give out what they do not have. I am not trying to make excuses for their excesses. All I am saying is that we should not have unrealistic expectations that cannot be met by our spouse.

Young men, you would have watched your mother do it all those days while growing up; from cooking to the laundry to running errands to shopping for the house and children always but bear in mind that she might have been a full housewife or your father must have insisted she doesn't work but just take care of the house. Here you are, married to a lady who works from 06:00am to 06:00pm or even 09:00pm; you know she can't afford to resign from that job due to the financial state of things in the family and finding another job is so difficult. She might even have opted to leave the job since she got married because of the stress but you kept telling her to hold on until she gets another replacement. Yet, you still expect her to always be available when you need her. You get so irritated when your meal is served late even if it happens once in a blue moon.

What about young wives? You know you got married to a man that is still trying to stand on his feet financially. You knew about it all along and still decided to marry him. All of a sudden, you are expecting the latest SUV from your husband because you saw your old classmate driving it. Where exactly do you want him to get it from? Your old class mate might be married to a multi-millionaire or would have even bought it herself. Avoid unrealistic expectations and apply wisdom always.

Financial Issues

We can't deny the fact that money is important to every aspect of our lives; our marital life inclusive. Enough of people pretending as if money doesn't matter. Money matters. Money is not the root of all evil. Rather, the love of money is the root of all evil. That's why one has to be financially capable before getting married. This doesn't mean that you must have millions in your bank account but at least, one or both partner should have a source of income. It doesn't necessarily have to be a nine to five job but something that brings in money.

Most couples are forced to live in their family house against their wish because they do not have money for house rent. It is so bad that some even reside in the wife's family house when their culture disallows this. Dear husbands, the demand of marriage is enough without having to add the ones that staying in such an environment creates. This is understandable and can be permitted if you are the only one living there or if it was handed to you as an inheritance by your parents.

It is worse when it is a typical African setting; the one that sees their son's wife as their wife. I know that those words of possession are sometimes used in a positive way to show affection, love and oneness but there are exceptions to this. At times, it is used to show that they can also ride over her and command her to do their wish. So our brother's wife becomes a cook for us permanently, a laundry woman, our nurse and macho woman. Funnily enough, the woman will not mind doing these things if she is respected and treated as a queen that she is but often times, she is insulted and treated like one that should be grateful that she found a husband. This is the sad reality of some African women that stay in family houses occupied by so many people. The woman bears it all as she doesn't want to complain to her husband or be seen as the one trying to divide their happy home. This is even more devastating if she is a housewife. They feel she should be overly engaged since their son and brother is the one working to get the money.

Be that as it may, there is always an exception to the general rule or school of thought. Some in-laws are so nice that they will practically worship their new wife and make her feel really loved but some aren't and you can't really tell if your people will do that to your wife or not. To be on the safe side, get a house of your own if you haven't built a personal house yet.

Some women are practically a shadow of themselves because of this and these issues happen because the money to pay for a house is unavailable. How can you ask your wife to stand for her right in the family house when they might be the one supplying the foodstuff? She would have to manage so that you can have what to eat and a roof over your head.

Don't joke with this. Lack of finance has killed joy in many marriages. A lady talked about her last pregnancy journey; she compared it to the first two times she got pregnant and preferred the last one. One might be tempted to think that her first journey through pregnancy should have been her most memorable, after all she was going to be a mother for the first time but it wasn't. I wanted to know what was so special about her third pregnancy and she said she wasn't working during her first and second pregnancy. Her husband was the only one working and they were just managing the little money he earned then. In fact, the bills were so much on him coupled with expectations from his family members. During that period, she would crave for certain things but won't be able to tell her husband. Did she want him to steal to supply those things? She didn't get enough baby wears as she wished. At times, she would understand that it was because of their low financial status but other times, she would get so frustrated and be very moody.

However, all of that changed when she got pregnant the third time as she was now running a successful business. She enjoyed her last pregnancy and it was so obvious as she glowed with excitement sharing her story of not being afraid of craving for things for the fear of not being able to buy them or not shopping adequately for her baby. One quick glance on her baby and I could see a well-dressed and fed baby. Do you know that it is so bad financially with some married couples that they have to beg for money to enable them feed their children? What about those that are told at their ante-natal care that they won't be able to deliver vaginally and will need to undergo caesarean section? Most ladies who break into uncontrollable tears do not do so because they are scared of the operation but because they don't have the money for it and are already thinking of how life will be with the arrival of a baby/babies and how they would have to deal with looking for money for an operation.

Don't think that this issue only affects the wife. The husband might be feeling moody and withdrawn. He might be crying secretly and seeing himself as a failure. Some women make it worse by reminding the man of what other husbands are doing for their families. He might have lost millions of naira in a business transaction and you might have warned him against that transaction but he was so sure of it.

For those who have not been able to see beyond the present, lack of finance can kill the joy in a marriage. Some women purposely start avoiding events where their married friends who are doing well would be found. Others might start feeling jealous of their younger siblings who got married to richer men. For some, they might start regretting the choice they made, especially if they left a man because he was poor without knowing that their husband's business will crash and leave them in a temporary state of poverty and that ex they left is now doing well financially.

That is why it is very important to have a saving scheme. Don't think that you can buy anything you want because you have the means to do so. Diversify your source of earning. With this present economy, it is not advisable to streamline your source of income to one business or job alone. Have you noticed that most people who are successful financially do not have one source of income? Don't sit idle and expect your rich relatives to take care of your family for you when you aren't handicapped or sick. A lot of people start getting angry and picking offence with their relatives when they cannot meet up with their financial demands.

Comments like these make no sense:
He refused to pay my rent.

Why can't he pay my son's fees?

Why didn't he handle the expenses for my daughter's birthday?

Why can't he buy foodstuff for my wife?

Frankly, nobody owes you anything most especially when you are married.

Another Dimension to This

The issue of finance being a killer of joy in marriages might not just be the absence of finance. It could be improper management of the available finances. Young couples must learn how to manage their finance and be meticulous in spending. This brings me to the area that might be a bit controversial for some people and I totally understand their reason. One cannot plan for what they have no idea about. You must be open about your finances. I know this is quite difficult for some people but your wife needs to know how much you earn and vice versa to enable both of you plan effectively.

For example, if the man earns N80,000 monthly and the woman earns N80,000 too, that means the total amount for that month is N160,000 aside other investments you both might be involved in. If this is the case, you shouldn't rent a house of N600,000 yearly. That amount is approximately your salary for four months as a couple. Won't you save up for other things? What about feeding and the children's expenses if any? The list goes on. A lot of young couples behave as if they are in competition with the older couples not knowing that they must have had their days of little beginning.

You must not put your child in a school of 1 million naira yearly because your friend's child attends that school. You might say, "After all, we both work in the same organization and I earn more than them" but you aren't aware of the other investments they might be doing or the hidden inheritance their parents left for them whereas you had to start life from the scratch as your parents left you with nothing. Your parents might have left you debts that you are still struggling to pay. Don't feel bad. They might have battled with a serious health challenge that caused them to sell off all they ever worked for and had to go into borrowing. It is not compulsory to go for a vacation abroad when you are not financially capable yet.

You might desire the latest car but for the mean time, who says you can't make do with a small car that is functional? Don't let people push you into what you aren't ready for financially. Cut your cloth according to your material, not according to your style. Your style might be more than your material. Spend wisely according to the income available to you, not according to your wants because human wants are insatiable.

There is no law that states that you must do an elaborate child dedication. As the name implies, child dedication simply means dedicating your child to God, the giver of children and every good gift. If you can afford an elaborate after-party, go ahead. Sincerely, I have no problem with that but if you know you cannot afford that and you are yet to return the money you borrowed for your wife's hospital bills when she gave birth, it won't be wise to incur another debt.

Cook meals you can afford as long as they are healthy and nourishing to the body. By the way, too much of meat isn't too good for your health. Don't think you must eat six pieces of meat in a meal just to show that you have arrived.

Buy wears you can afford. When you are beginning as a young couple on a low financial budget, you have no business with a lace worth N50,000 per yard except it was given to you as a gift; that means N200,000 for four yards. Can't that money be invested in something else? Refuse to compare your dressing with others. You can't tell if they bought the dresses themselves. I remember when I was to get married, my husband was given a long list. He was asked to buy a box and fill it with wrappers, different shades of gele, shoes, underwear and other costumes. I felt it was too much for him but I was told it was our culture and he wasn't forced to buy expensive ones. My husband got the best materials. He even insisted I go to the market with him to make my choice; after all, I would be the one wearing them. As a result of my cultural practice, I was always changing clothes after my marriage, not necessarily because I just bought them but because I had them before I got married.

Learn to manage your finances efficiently and effectively to avoid running into money issues that can tamper with the joy in marriages if not well handled.

Not Understanding Personality Traits

I discussed personality traits in chapter one and I would relate it to how it can destroy joy in marriages. If you knew your husband talks too much and you went ahead to marry him, you should be able to accommodate that aspect of him. There is no point trying to change him by force. The best you can do is letting him know that some sensitive things you tell him must remain with him and if that isn't working, you need to know the kind of things to tell him.

I heard of a young woman that got married to a talkative man. She told him the sex of their baby during her first pregnancy and before she knew it, everyone in her husband's office knew that she was expecting a baby boy. She got angry as expected but decided to handle things better next time. I don't support her keeping the sex of their baby a secret from her husband but she had to since he saw absolutely nothing wrong with telling his colleagues. For the next pregnancy, she kept her mouth shut on the sex of the baby. Her husband was a typical sanguine, always wanting to talk.

Your wife might be a typical melancholy and will love to have things done perfectly well. Understand her for who she is. There is no point screaming at her and telling her she analyses things too much like a dummy. You should be happy that she is there to analyse things that meticulously if you are the type that likes to take hasty decisions.

Failure to understand the personality traits of your partner can kill the joy in marriage as no one likes to be called a dummy. Most women do not like the sex of their unborn child being announced that soon into pregnancy.

Lack of Respect

I won't limit this to only the wife respecting the husband. This is more of mutual respect. In as much as it is expected of a wife to respect her husband, the husband also has to respect his wife.

Men love to be respected. Women, you must have heard this countless times and I guess you might have gotten tired of hearing it but we keep saying it because it is the truth. Men love to be respected. Give him his due respect as the man of the house, your husband, father of your children, and the one who married you. Even if you married him depending on your culture, he still deserves to be treated with full respect as a human being.

Men, it is much easier for women to respect their husbands than it is for men to respect their wives but you can be an exception. Respect your wife and let her know that you respect her. Enough of always demanding respect selfishly. Everyone deserves to be respected, including your wife. Let it reflect in the way you talk to her and treat her. When you see a man's family insulting the wife, most of the times it is because the man has not placed her highly before them and let them know that he respects her. Real men say, "I respect my wife and if you want me to be nice to you and tolerate you being around, you must also respect my wife." No one is saying you should kneel down or shake when she is around. It's far from that. When you respect your wife, it will reflect in the things you do even in her absence. It will also reflect in how you listen to her suggestions and make decisions that affect her.

If you respect your wife, you won't wake up one day and suddenly say, "My mother is coming to live with us and that is final" or "My brothers have gotten admission into the university and they are coming to live here with us until they graduate. You have to get used to it." Knowing that the house is also her home and space, you will discuss with her instead and try to make her see reasons with your choice. You won't make it look like you have already concluded on the matter and just coming to inform her. You will seek her opinion before taking major decisions. Your reason for wanting them to live with you might be genuine and as a result of financial constraint but you can do it in a better way. You can say something like, "I know we agreed that no one will live with us for the time being but mummy is terribly sick and you know I'm her only child or my other siblings are out of the country. John and James have gotten admission into the university and the financial responsibility is all on me. I didn't know they will both be admitted the same year. We are also building and have other commitments. I can't afford to pay their fees, accommodation, take care of their feeding and transport. At least, if they are here, I will only have to worry about their transport fare. Please, I know this is quite difficult for you but I will be so glad if you can understand. If they give you any issue, you can correct them. After all, they are like your younger siblings and if you can't handle it, get me involved. "If you got married to a good woman, she won't be able to resist it and if she needs a little more time to process it, give it to her.

It is very easy to know a man who respects his wife and a man who doesn't; the same with the women. Your marriage will be heaven on earth if you both love and respect each other.

Wrong Communication Patterns

Another killer of joy in marriage is wrong communication patterns. If you do not learn how to communicate rightly, it would affect your marriage negatively. Communication goes beyond saying what you have to say. A lot of married couples are suffering in their marriages and they end up bottling a lot of things that should be shared with each other. They get frustrated in the process. The power of communicating effectively cannot be over-emphasized. Some married couples are just talking without communicating.

There will be times in your marriage when you would have some unpleasant things to tell your spouse. You might be so offended that you just want to explode and pour out everything at once irrespective of how your spouse will feel. In as much as your anger might be justified depending on what transpired, you have to put yourself together before speaking or wait until you are a bit calm. The danger of saying what you want to say in that mood is that the other person might end up being defensive and both of you could quarrel or drift apart the more instead of actually communicating.

Since we have established a fact that wrong communication patterns can kill joy in marriages, how then can we communicate effectively with our spouse for maximum result?
Before I suggest ways of communicating effectively, let's look at some mistakes new couples make while communicating.

— Shouting at the other person.

— Interrupting the person who is speaking.

— Walking out while the other person is still pouring out his/her heart.

— Body languages that show you are not listening.

— Browsing through your phone while the other person is talking.

— Choosing a wrong time to communicate sensitive issues.

— Being tactless.

— Not considering the outcome of the discussion.

How to Communicate Effectively

Below are some ways that can help new couples communicate effectively.

— **Think before you speak out**

You might be in a hurry to pour out your mind to your spouse but be very sure you have pondered on what you want to say. There is no need spilling words about things you aren't sure of. For example, you were driving past your husband's office and you saw him talking with a lady. You should be able to find out who the lady was in a nice way that doesn't suggest you are already accusing him. The lady might be a colleague or an old friend he ran into. Before you go to him and angrily tell him he is cheating on you, think deeply. Most times, young wives create problems for themselves because they keep listening to the wrong people who always tell them that no man can be trusted.

Think of the possible outcome of what you want to say before saying it. This doesn't necessarily mean you should keep quiet because the outcome won't be favourable. It only means that you need to look for a more comfortable time and think of ways to apply more tact to what you have to say.

— State Your Points Clearly.

Let your partner not guess what you really mean. Be very clear in stating your points. If you want to communicate about the attitude of your husband towards you recently, state that clearly. Don't start talking about how your friend's husband is treating your friend like a queen that people wonder if he is under magical influence. That is a wrong way to pass a message across. No one likes to be compared unfavourably. Simply state what you have to say in clear terms that your husband can easily understand.

Life is difficult enough with people trying to make ends meet. Don't make it more difficult by expecting your partner to be able to read your mind especially if you just got married to this person and he/she has not studied you enough to understand your non-verbal communication.

For example, your elder sister's husband is celebrating his 40th birthday and you need your husband to attend the function with you. Simply go ahead and ask for his company. Tell him that you will love him to be there with you for the function. It is normal for some men to refuse initially. Instead of getting angry, engage his emotions by saying some nice things about the man. You can say, "He was the one that helped me talk to my dad to accept you when my dad was initially being cold about accepting you. Remember he really supported us during our wedding. He is such a nice man."

Some wives might tell their husband this, "My elder sister invited me to her husband's 40th birthday" and the husbands might respond, "Okay, my dear. That is good. You can attend it." Meanwhile what you really wanted was his company to the birthday party. Don't assume he should know he has to be in that party. Darling young wife, not every man knows these things. Some men grew up in families where people do not make a big deal out of birthdays. He might be the type that sees birthdays as a time for only sober reflection and nothing else.

The men are not left out of this. You might want your wife to prepare melon soup for dinner. Simply tell her lovingly, "My love, please can you cook melon soup? It has been long I had that" instead of beating around the bush and telling her of how you ate melon soup in a friend's house. She might be thinking that since you ate melon soup in a friend's house the day before, she should give you variety by cooking stew; meanwhile, you don't mind eating melon soup again. As little as this looks, it can cause problems in the home.

While communicating, clearly state your points.

— Avoid Talking at The Same Time

When your spouse is talking, listen. It is not the time to shout or start talking. This is why marriage is only for the mature. Maturity here is not about age per se. Let them round off with their speech before you say what you have to say. The danger of talking at the same time is that no one is actually listening to the other person and the main aim of communication which is passing information has been defeated.

One way to help you avoid talking at the same time is to listen to know where you went wrong or get the information, not to react immediately. You can get a pen and paper to jot some points you want to make reference to when it gets to your turn to speak in case you think you might forget what you have to say.

— Care About How Your Spouse Will Feel

If you really love a person, you will care about how he/she will feel. It is not right to say, "I don't give a damn about how you feel, I just want to tell you my mind and that's all." If you are fond of saying this, it would get to a point where the other person will not want to listen to what you have to say because you do not care about how the other person will feel. We should always remember that the goal in communicating with our spouse is to pass a message across, not to act as if we are enemies.

— Choose the Right Words/Be Tactful

Being tactful and choosing the right words goes hand in hand. Remember the last point before this was on caring about how your spouse will feel. One way to achieve this is by being tactful with the words you use.

Your wife's mother might have over-stepped her boundaries in your home and you want her to leave soon to avoid further issues but you need to know how best to communicate that to your wife. You cannot just tell your wife, "Your mother is foolish to think she can control my home. Do I look like her weak husband? The next time she tries this with me, I will give her a slap." This is a no-no. Depending on your wife's tolerance level, she can throw abuses at you for insulting her mother and also involving her father. That's how trouble begins.

Being tactful means that you can still say what you have to say but you choose your words carefully. In the example above, you can still pass the message of not liking your mother in-law's behaviour by saying, "My wife, I appreciate the fact that mummy came to help us take care of junior but I sincerely do not like the way she talks to me. Even my parents will not talk to me that way. You have to talk to her to respect me as your husband."

— Choose The Right Time and Venue

Your husband cannot come back from work tired, hungry and exhausted and you suddenly bring up the discussion of how he has not yet given you the money for the lace you asked him of. It is a wrong time. Most men are not always set for a discussion of any sort when they are hungry. How much more being tired, hungry and exhausted? You need to put a hold to demanding the money for the lace. Wait until he has eaten, rested and gotten back his energy. If not, you might be wasting your time or he might yell at you such that you might start wondering if he wasn't the one that promised the money for the lace.

You have to choose the venue rightly. You cannot go to your husband's office and start screaming in the name of communicating with him. You have to wait for him to come back home. Also, you cannot be in your in-law's house and want to discuss very sensitive issues; issues that you know might create a scene, attract attention or an issue that you are not really sure of how your spouse would respond.

— Avoid Calling Names

If the discussion is getting so heated with no obvious head way, it might be time to pause instead of calling each other names. Before you got married, you might have seen or heard couples yelling and calling themselves derogatory names that you cannot help but wonder if they were forced to get married. Do not repeat that in your home. Calling your husband a foolish man won't solve the issue at home. Calling your wife a slut or a nagging fool won't solve the issue. It would rather make things worse. Control the words that come out of your mouth when you are angry.

— Avoid So Much Lecturing

Stating the issue at hand is different from sitting an adult down for hours lecturing them. Anything that is done too much can be annoying and frustrating. At that time, you could lose their attention as they are already tired.

— Watch Body Language

This can help you know when they are becoming bored during the discussion and help you conclude. It also helps you know when they are finding your words really offensive and you have to adjust or choose your words wisely.

Another dimension to this is that it can help you know if your spouse is understanding you. From the way they look at you, nod their heads, roll their eyes, smile, frown, or laugh.

— Be A Good Listener

This is very important and that is why I decided to make it the last on this list. Don't always be in a hurry to speak. Learn to listen as well. It is really comforting and encouraging when your spouse knows that they have your undivided attention. You might have to switch off your phone or keep it away while having an important conversation with your spouse. It is not the time to keep answering every call and surfing the Internet. Give your partner your full attention. Most issues that occur in marriages are as a result of couples who do not listen to each other. The woman knows the man won't listen and so she has someone else, sometimes a male friend that she runs to always to pour out her heart and the man does same. If care is not taken, they might begin to develop affection for these other people that act as good listeners. That's how emotional affairs grow into adultery.

It's not good for another lady aside a man's wife to know so much about his family up to when his wife gets pregnant, the last fight they had, and the wife's bad behaviours. Why not learn the art of listening to yourselves and communicating effectively?

Having studied some points that can kill joy in marriages, we should know that if we avoid those things and have our anchor on God who is the creator of marriage, we can be sure of a home filled with joy and marital bliss.

Love Birds Exercise 4.

•Are there some things your spouse is doing that is killing the joy in your marriage? Write them down and lovingly draw your spouse's attention to it.

• Do you spend more time on your phone than you spend with your spouse? If yes, are you willing to correct that?

• Make a list of your communication patterns with your spouse in the last one year. Has it been effective enough?

• Train your tongue to be shut while your spouse is speaking so you can listen attentively and respond with maturity.

CHAPTER FIVE

DEALING WITH DELAYS

No one likes delay. Having a desire and waiting to see that desire become a reality is not easy. No one likes to wait, especially in a setting that suggests that people experiencing one delay or the other aren't prayerful enough. Most religious organizations do that unknowingly. It is common to hear pastors or officiating ministers say things like, "You are coming for your baby's dedication in nine months." They make it sound as if the baby would be dedicated to God in church the minute it is born.

I am happy that most ministers are beginning to notice the untold pressure they unconsciously mount on people. I once heard a minister say, "Go and have it the way you want" and went on to tell the family of the man and friends to desist from being a womb watcher. Allow them have some space and if you think there is something wrong, pass the message tactfully.

I decided to write on delay in conception first because this is an obvious need but not necessarily the most pressing need. A couple might be trusting God for healing of a deadly disease but because the disease can't be seen, people might not really know or pay attention to it. Once a couple have lived together for over a year without a child, no one cares to know if it is deliberate or not. You would notice a lot of side talks. Others might be so bold to say it to your face regardless of how you will feel. You can be sick and hide it as a couple but you can't be trusting God for a child and hide it except you both relocate to a place where no one knows about your history and start life afresh. Sadly, if you decide to adopt, some people with myopic mindset will still not let you be.

It is a phase in one's life that people dread. Children come from God as clearly stated in Psalm 127:3 "Lo, children are an heritage of the Lord and the fruit of the womb is his reward." Some couples are under serious stress and if the man isn't strong, they don't mind suggesting a new wife for him. Some might advise the man to try outside. Ironically, the reason for the delay could come from the man and once that is noticed, the tune begins to change. Most people in this part of the world automatically think that the reason for any delay in conception must come from the woman.

What Should I Do When There Is a Delay in Conception

— **Give Yourself Time**

Before you start running around in search of solution, be sure there is a problem. What do I mean by this? You might not be doing some things right; some ladies do not know how to count their ovulation. Some might not be living in the same town with their spouse. Some might be trying to get over the stress of the wedding. This is the reason medical practitioners suggest that a couple try for at least a year before seeking medical attention if unsuccessful and six months if the lady is above 35 years of age.

Some couples get married and in just two months, they start getting so worried about not being able to get pregnant.

— **Seek help**

The first type of help you need is spiritual help. I sincerely wish I had this information when I got married newly. You need to spend time with the giver of children and find out some deep truths which only Him can reveal. What does God want us to do? Even if we are to seek medical attention, how soon and who should we see? Life itself is spiritual and I have come to know that the spiritual controls the physical. It is also important to know God's mind over the issue. Is this what God is allowing to teach us something? Is the delay spiritual or does it need medical attention?

While seeking spiritual help, be very sensitive to what God will be saying to you. This is also a time to pray targeted prayers, not general prayers like, "Lord, give us children." What if God has already given you children but the answers to your prayers are being held by strange forces? You need to command those demonic forces to take their hands off your children.

Daniel in the Bible kept praying and God told him he already heard his prayer from the very day he made up his mind to seek God's face concerning that issue but the answers were withheld and Angel Michael was released to make sure the answer got to Daniel. I have seen some couples experiencing delay in conception and because of the unbearable pressure from people, they decide to run around seeking medical help whereas the issue is spiritual. It's just like using a key that is meant for a bike to start a car. Frustration would definitely set in and one might get tired along the way.

There was a couple who experienced delay in conception for over six years after marriage. They kept running from one hospital to another in search of help. They even opted for In Vitro Fertilization (IVF) but their effort was fruitless; that was when they decided to seek God's face and hear his mind on the issue. They got to discover that it was a spiritual attack and obeyed the instructions of their pastor and few months after, they had their first baby and others followed. Today, they are blessed with three beautiful children. What if they didn't take out time to seek God's face? Let God not be your last resort. Make Him your first go-to person because it will save you from needless pains and headaches. Frankly, the time of seeking God's face might not be pleasant. It could involve taking off days from your place of work or secluding yourself from people but the result cannot be compared to the discomfort.

You can seek medical help if you feel led to do so. This doesn't in any way suggest that you do not have faith. God can direct you to a specialist and in a short while, the issue of delay in conception becomes a thing of the past. If you decide to seek medical help, don't rely only on the information the doctor and health practitioners give you. Do your research as well and ask questions on any area you need clarity on. Keep to all your appointments and adhere strictly to medical instructions.

— Be There for Each Other

This is a time to prove your genuine love for one another. This isn't the time to point accusing fingers to either side of the families or yourselves. Whatever decision you make, you still need to be there for each other.

If you both have decided to seek spiritual help first, do it together if you both can. It is understandable if one partner doesn't join in the fasting because of health challenge or can't go to church to pray constantly because of the nature of their jobs but just displaying a nonchalant attitude or thinking it is the woman's duty alone isn't encouraging at all. This is usually the norm in most societies. We find women crying to God for children in church especially in programmes organized for waiting parents while the man is at home surfing the net. Won't the children bear your name? Won't they be yours as well? This is the time you need to prove you love each other.

I once heard the interview of a couple who waited before having children and the man said he made sure he accompanied his wife for every medical check-up and appointment. The investigative test for couples trying to conceive are usually more invasive for the women than the men. From the Hysterosalphingogram (HSG) to hydrotubation, to Intrauterine Insemination (IUI) or In Vitro Fertilization (IVF) as the case may be; all these can have a negative effect on the woman if she has no strong support system. What greater support system can a woman have other than her husband's support? How sweet it will be for both of you to go for medical check-ups together, holding each other's hands as you receive injections. Instead of yelling, "Woman, you fear so much. Take the damn injection and let's get out of here." How sweet it will be if you say something like, "I'm here love. I got you. This won't last forever. Hold me and look away from the injection; think of our little babies." I have discovered that couples who go through delays and come out stronger do have a special and rare kind of bond.

Being there for each other might entail you praying fervently for your spouse while he or she is wheeled in for a surgical operation if need be, being their nurse until they recover and if your work permits it, taking time out to be with them at moments when they need you most.

— Protect Your Wife

Some in-laws understand when there is a delay in child bearing and pray from a distance and if they have any meaningful thing to suggest, they do it respectfully. However, some will not mind tormenting the wife due to her inability to conceive. It is at this time that you need to be a man and protect your wife. Anyone that truly loves you will also love the woman that you picked out of the numerous women in the world. Most times, I wonder if these family members think the woman isn't bothered. Do they think the woman's family isn't also bothered? Wise people know that mounting pressure and stress is not good for a person who is trying to conceive as it can alter her ovulation and menstrual cycle.

A man had to warn his sister never to visit him again because she kept using hurtful words on his wife, calling her a man and all sorts of derogatory names. Funnily enough, she got married and experienced delay and her mouth got shut. At this time, her brother's wife that she called a man had given birth to four children.

There was a man who went outside because he felt his wife was the problem. A desperate lady took advantage of the situation and in less than four years of dating her, she gave him two children but it was later discovered that none was his. She only saw desperation written all over him and used it to her advantage since she knew he was rich and very liberal with his finances.

Be there for each other at every step in every way possible. Barrenness cannot last forever. The Bible says in Exodus 23:26a, "There shall nothing cast their young, nor be barren in the land." Hold unto God's word as you continually honour your marriage vow.

Sieve Suggestions Carefully

Don't allow desperation send you to an early grave or give you incurable disease that the issue of delay in conception becomes a child's play when compared to that. A lot of people will suggest a whole lot of things for you to do and take. In as much as many of those suggestions would be coming from people who mean well, think thoroughly before doing it. People have complicated the issue due to the numerous concoctions they have taken. I wept when I heard of a lady who was experiencing deadly pains and discomfort because of the things she took to help her conceive.

Know that some people will take advantage of your situation to suggest some things that do not work to you in order to swindle you of your money especially if they know you are rich and look very desperate. You must have heard of some ladies that fake pastors sleep with under the umbrella of cleansing them of the evil spirit to enable them get married or conceive. If you don't take care, you would spend all your money such that you start begging for money to train the kids when they finally come or you might end up becoming polluted spiritually because of the wrong places you have visited in search of solutions.

Even if the advice they are giving to you is good, you need to know if the timing is okay. Someone might be suggesting IVF to you but are you prepared financially, physically, emotionally and otherwise? If you think you need more time to think about it, don't let people rush you. Remember that you will be the one going through the whole invasive procedures, not anyone else.

Also, what worked for them might not work for you because your physiological make-up is different from theirs. Be very sure of a treatment plan before you go ahead with it. The bitter truth is once your life ends, you won't be able to fulfil your dream of becoming a parent. Avoid self-medication. There are some medications that must only be taken with close supervision of a fertility doctor, gynaecologist or health practitioner. Don't put your life at risk by doing things that are harmful to your body just because you don't want people to feel bad or feel you are doing nothing about the situation. You know better if you are concerned about it or not. No one can claim to be more concerned than the ones in that shoe. They might not be aware of the things you are doing behind the scene and you are not under any obligation to inform the world of what you are doing to become a parent.

Some people fail to acknowledge these set of couples; they already have a child but need more. Some people make it look like they already have one and so they shouldn't be worried about not being able to get pregnant after a year or more years of trying. You cannot tell this set of couples that they have no right to worry. That is being so insensitive to their plight. They won't worry if they decided to have only one child but if that wasn't their plan, they are bound to get worried.

Let me kindly appeal to couples who haven't struggled with getting pregnant to be careful of the things they tell those who are trying to get pregnant. I've heard such couples cut off from friends who aren't mindful of the things they say. The stress of trying to get pregnant is enough and they don't need any more stress from people who are so insensitive. Don't say you mean no harm. It's not a matter of meaning no harm but knowing what to say. It is insensitive to speak of how fertile you are in a way that shows superiority when speaking with those who haven't gotten pregnant. Can I shock you? Most times, it has nothing to do with how fertile you are but God's faithfulness.

A lady had three children and desperately needed a fourth child. Her husband told her that he was okay with the three they had but she kept insisting that they see a gynaecologist to find out why she hasn't been able to get pregnant again after the third child. As they examined her, they told her to be extremely grateful to God that she already has three children because from what they were seeing, that was nothing short of a miracle. She left that hospital with a new approach to life and a heart filled with gratitude. Do you know that so many couples still trusting God for children are very fit to have children? It might be more of a spiritual issue or God preparing a special seed for them.

Someone told a friend about the money she had spent so far on fertility treatment and her friend's reply was shocking. "That money can build a small house. Why are you wasting it on such futile steps when I am here looking for money? Well, thank God I don't have to go through that." Those insensitive comments are so wrong. Firstly, it is a problem to your friend and that is why she is spending on it. You might not have to spend to become a parent but if you are spending money to get a job or get cured from a disease, then it is the same thing. People spend on what they consider important to them. Secondly, why do you think it is a futile spending? Even if you feel it will not work for her, you can tell her that in a better way.

Lastly, no one is obliged to give you money, especially when the person isn't a family member. Work hard for your money and don't monitor how others spend their money. Did you get pregnant on your wedding night? Congratulations!

However, never mock or look down on those still believing God to conceive.

Develop A Shock Absorber

Regardless of if you are experiencing a delay in conception or not, everyone needs a shock absorber in life. When experiencing a delay in conception, you need it more because you would hear a lot of things from people; people that you think should understand better or those very close to you. You must not take everything to mind. They are probably speaking from their myopic mindset and limited knowledge. People might be very blunt and won't mind asking why you still have a flat stomach but you don't have to come home crying always. Don't let it get to you. Life always has a way of teaching people how to keep shut if they have nothing nice to say and when they eventually understand, they keep quiet. The fact that you see your monthly period and ovulate does not mean you might not have a little challenge in getting pregnant. Ask those who are trying to conceive and they will tell you that they never saw it coming. More so, these insensitive comments might be coming from those who aren't yet married or those who didn't experience delay. Those who experienced delay are very careful of what they say to people who are trying to conceive.

A lady who got married quite early was unable to conceive two years into the marriage. She disliked visiting her mother in-law but her husband kept telling her that his mother won't give her issues as she also waited for years before having him who is her first child. When she decided to go and see her mother-in-law after a long time, the discussion they had made her very happy and relaxed. Her mother-in-law told her of how she waited for almost seven years before having her husband and told her that she doesn't wish those years for her but she should know that no one will disturb her and she has the full support of her in-laws. Today, she has five children. Delay is never denial. It wasn't up to three months after that discussion with her mother-in-law that she took in for her first child and her first child wasn't up to one year when she took in again.

You might consider her very lucky and be upset that the people you expect to be on your side are tearing you down. I totally understand you, dear young wife. You might have the support of just your husband and your in-laws might be calling you terrible names and sending you hateful text messages. There is nothing you can do to stop them from being who they are or who they want to be but all you can do is to make sure it doesn't get that much to you because if it does, you could develop severe health challenges in the process.

Forgive people. Like I have earlier said, some of them don't know what they are saying. There was a lady who always mocked others who were married without children because she felt it couldn't happen to her and was extremely careless in her choice of words. She got married eventually and couldn't conceive after two years plus. That was when she started calling her friends to apologize. She got to understand life better. Know that some people making the insensitive comments are not an authority in knowing why people have delay in conception. Simply forgive them and move on.

Sometimes, you might have to give some people their own pill and let them have a taste of it. I heard a funny story which I will love to share here. One lady went to church and typical of most Nigerian churches, they told everyone to hold the hands of a person of their choice and pray for them. Someone walked up to this lady, held her hands and started shouting, "Oh God, give her a child." Her voice was so loud and the lady didn't like it. So she decided to also increase her own voice, "Oh God, give her a husband." The other lady's voice reduced immediately and they both went silent in their prayers. She got to understand that the other person could also shout and she had a need too.

In summary, have a shock absorber. Let people's comment not take you unawares. Know that some people do not know how to talk. It might not have anything to do with you; they just don't know how to talk.

Protect Your Space

Trying to conceive for years can be very overwhelming especially if your type of infertility is described as unknown. The last thing you need is additional stress. I am not suggesting that you shut people out because you will still need people but if the people in your space are those that constantly laugh at you, always narrowing the discussion to childbirth and making it look like you are less of a human being, it's time to protect your space from them. You are not fighting or quarrelling with them but you are simply doing what is best for you. Despite the fact that you keep telling them that their constant insensitive remarks are having negative effects on you, they won't want to understand. Some might even term you as jealous.

A lady had a serious medical procedure as regards fertility and she couldn't go to work since she was told by the doctors to rest adequately but as soon as she switched on her phone, she saw a message from a friend who was pregnant at the time and organizing her birthday. She was inviting her for the birthday and insisting she comes if not, she won't be happy with her. So she had to go for that birthday party and almost broke down for not adhering to the doctor's instructions. Well, she learnt from that experience and decided not to put her life in danger again in order to please people. Protect your space by all means. You might have to relocate depending on how bad the effect of the delay is on you. A lady was talking about her early days of marriage and how she experienced delay in conception for a year but the effect was so much on them that they decided to relocate. Amazingly, she got pregnant the year she relocated. Before then, each time the pastor in church requests for those trusting God for children to come out, some hyper-active people would be looking for her and hurrying her up. One day, she had to react. "I've been married for only few months. My husband isn't always in town and I haven't cried to you that I am looking for children desperately. For goodness sake, it is only five months and you don't even know if we have decided to wait for one year." When she couldn't take it any longer, they decided to relocate.

You know the people that can stress you and the ones that genuinely want the best for you. You should know who to allow in your space to protect your sanity. You are not under compulsion to listen to every discussion. Know when to thank people and tell them it's enough. Don't let people dictate what happens in your home because of any delay; if not they can turn to the god of your home and ultimately ruin your home. The danger of not having a firm hold over your space is that anyone can suggest things to you and if you aren't strong, you would fall prey to demonic advice.

Develop The Virtue of Patience.

A song writer once said, "After you have known all you can, just stand." The fact that you are praying or seeking medical help doesn't mean the desired change would come immediately. For some, it might be immediate but others might have to wait a little longer. If you are a strong Christian, you would know that patience is a virtue. Refuse to give up on the verge of your breakthrough. If you aren't a Christian or if the search for the fruit of the womb has caused you to wander far from the truth, you can rededicate your life to God. Invite Jesus into your life as your personal Lord and Saviour and attend any Bible believing church around you. If God can open our eyes to see the reason for the delay, you would start thanking God. He could have seen a danger that He is trying to avert or preparing your womb to birth world changers and kingdom giants. Dear husbands, this isn't the time to sleep outside. Dear wives, don't be tempted to get pregnant outside and put the responsibility on your husband. No amount of pressure should make you do that. It isn't worth it at all. Do you think the pressure will reduce once you give birth? You will be shocked to know that it will continue if you allow yourself to be constantly pressurized. You might finally give birth to a girl child and they start pressurizing you for a boy child or for the next child.

A man got married to his beautiful wife and was enjoying his home. It didn't really bother him that they were yet to become parents but his friends started mounting pressure on him and suddenly, he became so impatient and couldn't wait again. He picked a second wife and his wife was confirmed pregnant the same month the new woman came into the home. She bore six children while the second wife had two children. Reports had it that until he died, he kept regretting that move of impatience. No one is saying that waiting is the easiest thing to do but if you see yourselves as a team, you won't take decisions that are not in the best interest of both of you. Imagine how the man in this story must have felt when his long awaited testimony came the same month he took the wrong step. No one knows the stress he might have gone through keeping two wives in the same house. Of course, he must have had no choice but to tolerate the excesses; after all, he brought it upon himself.

Don't take decisions in a haste. Sit down and carefully examine the advantages and disadvantages of that decision. Think of the long-term effect as well, not just the immediate gratification. Even if you decide to adopt, you need to be sure that is what you really want to do and be guided properly on how best to go about it. Don't let anyone rush you because they won't be there when you start reaping the fruits of any wrong step you take. Some mistakes cannot be undone; you just have to live with them for the rest of your life.

Maintain Your Joy

It is not surprising that for some couples, as soon as they stop worrying about conception and occupy their minds with other things, conception takes place. It is such a pity that some people have decided to make themselves womb watchers. I once read some people's opinion on Facebook and I laughed when some said a marriage without children lacks joy. That is hasty generalization. If actually children are the only pre-requisite for joy in marriages, then marriages which are blessed with children should be the happiest but most times, that isn't the case. In my journey of being a marriage mentor, I've handled cases of depression in marriages and some of them are blessed with children. Some are even abused physically, emotionally and otherwise and are just there because of their children.

Joy comes from God. Work on your mentality and the way you view things. If you trust God enough, never allow yourself to be moody. Don't act as if life has been so unfair to you. Let the atmosphere in your home be filled with joy. So far, what has worrying done for you? Most women still believing God for the fruit of the womb draw the attention they receive to themselves. They look so distant, unkempt, and perpetually moody such that people think it is because of that. I perfectly understand but try to be happy.

When you notice that you are about to go into depression, quickly switch on to those godly and beautiful things that make you happy. It might be listening to Christian music, watching comedy videos, going to YouTube to watch videos that are of interest to you or any other thing that makes life fun for you.

A lot of women have made their homes so uncomfortable for everybody including their husbands. Because they are two years in marriage without a child, all their discussions at home must always be centred on children. They make their husbands afraid of coming back home knowing he would hear the same old story.

Live Your Life

You should not put your life on hold due to a delay. This might restrict your movement and you would have to decline some offers. It is not advisable to live in different cities as you need to be together and meet as husband and wife often. However, you shouldn't be idle. Some women are practically doing nothing. They are postponing everything until they become parents- no future ambition, career drive or dream. There was a lady who was trying to conceive for three years. At first, she was doing nothing. She was only sitting at home and feeling sorry for herself but thank God she advised herself and became gainfully employed. She later gave birth to triplets. How would only her husband's salary have sustained them? Since she was already gainfully employed, they were able to adequately take care of their precious gifts from God.

I know that some naive and even educated people might be saying some hurtful words in your absence. Some might say it to your face, "Let her keep being a career woman when she has no child. What would they use all the money they are making for?" Well, you shouldn't listen to them. If you decide to eventually settle for fertility treatments, you would understand why you need money because they are not cheap and even if you don't decide on fertility treatments, won't you pay your bills like food, transportation, rent, building project and upkeep of family members? When you finally become a parent, won't you take care of your children? Money is needed to do that. A lot of people on your neck to have children might not get your baby/babies diapers or cloths.

If you do not want to accept a paid employment because you feel it will add up to your stress level or take you away from your spouse when you really need to spend time together, that is understandable but by all means, refuse to put your life on hold. These days, there are other things that can be done from the comfort of your home. You can also enrol for further studies and complete courses online without being physically present in those locations.

It won't be nice to have experienced a delay in conception and start running around for financial help when the baby/babies arrive.

Financial Breakthrough Delay

The same principles applied when experiencing a delay in conception can also be applied here. Women are also advised to save. The man should be able to provide for the family but that doesn't mean you should spend your own money carelessly as a wife. You might have to take up the financial responsibility for a while in case something goes wrong with the finances of your husband.

Some couples might not be experiencing delay in conception but are yet to get out of poverty. This might have happened immediately after they got married. Some could be wondering if their own marriage brought them disfavour unlike what the Bible stated in Proverbs 18:22. "Whosoever findeth a wife findeth a good thing, and obtaineth favour of the Lord." You have to deal with this spiritually and physically because faith without work is dead. As you pray for open doors financially, also know how to sustain it. A lot of women tend to lose respect for their husbands once he can no longer meet up his financial obligations. They insult him, speak to him disrespectfully and go as far as serving him unhealthy meals. Let's get this right. If everyone in the family is eating the same unhealthy meal as that is all the family can afford at the time, it is okay but eating a different meal and serving your husband a different meal just because he lost his job is not good at all.

Stand by him during this period of financial delay. The hardship could be so bad that the only way out is selling the car that makes movement easy for the family. Men go through a lot of personal challenges. At this time of his life, he might be so unsure of himself and you need to massage his ego. You know what needs to be bought in the house.

Don't wait for him to ask you for money to do that. Do it quietly and don't make a big deal out of it. You should be grateful to God that as his wife, you can still take charge of the home before he bounces back

I understand that it might not be funny but remember that this is just a phase and things will definitely get better.

Salvation Delay

It is possible to have gotten married to your spouse while you both were unbelievers and everything was going on well until one person saw the light. It is much easier if both of you received the gift of salvation together but sometimes, this doesn't happen. One person would have to stand in the gap praying earnestly for the salvation of the other person. It can be tiring but you must not give up. Ask the Holy Spirit for grace when you get overwhelmed and want to throw in the towel. Think of the joy of salvation you are enjoying and let that motivate you to keep praying for the salvation of your spouse.

Love Birds Exercise 5.

• Are you experiencing delay in any aspect of your marriage? If yes, what have you done to ensure it doesn't affect your marriage negatively?

• What specific word of God are you holding on to while you take the necessary actions to get out of such delays?

• If you are experiencing a delay in conception, are you there for each other? If no, make a new commitment to be there for each other until the kids come and forever.

• If you're experiencing financial delay, both of you should strategically look into ways to diversify your source of income or adjust your spending?

CHAPTER SIX

SEX IN MARRIAGE

*S*ex is one of the ways to fulfil one of the intentions of marriage which is pleasure. However, it is still one area where a lot of young couples struggle in. The enemy magnifies sex before marriage and that's why you find a lot of unmarried people engaging in it but once they get married and have been given the license to have it as many times as they desire, they are either too busy or do not know how to satisfy their spouses. For some, especially wives, they feel they are now married and do not really care about the sexual needs of their husbands. While some reasons are genuine, either they are pregnant and trying to adjust to what it is happening in their bodies or some just gave birth through caesarean operation and are trying to heal, others are nonchalant and believe that no matter how you satisfy a man sexually, a man will cheat. I see that as hasty generalization because sex isn't the only reason a man cheats.

HOW CAN I MAKE SEX PLEASURABLE?

Talk About Sex

Before you ask if sex is a big deal, let me start by saying it is. Welcome to the institution of marriage. Of course, marriage is not all about sex but sex is one of the things to be enjoyed in a marriage. Just as you talk about other things that you think are important to the marriage, also talk about sex as it is also important to a marriage. A man doesn't just want sex; a man needs sex. The thing with talking about sex is that it lets you know what your partner fancies sexually. For those who got married as virgins, I accept it might be totally awkward for you but as time goes on, you will adjust. That's if you are open to adjusting, not just wishing you adjust.

Prepare Your Mind

It is good to prepare your spouse's mind during the day about sex, especially if it is going to take place at night. You can send your husband loving messages telling him that you can't wait to have him and warn him against exerting all his energy at work and vice versa. Calling each other during the day and saying nothing but sweet words can build up the anticipation of what is about to happen. Leaving your spouse with loving words in the parlour before you leave for work is also a good way to prepare their mind.

Apart from preparing their minds, work on your own mind too. Psych yourself up and get excited that you have been blessed with someone to give your body lovingly to for life until death do you both part.

Help Your Wife Out

Men, let me speak to you; your wife is not a Jackie or someone that doesn't get tired. If you get back from work before her and notice that dinner isn't served, you can do it. You can help her wash the dishes so that she doesn't come back home tired and exhausted and still have to do all the chores before going to bed.

This is not in any way trying to compare wives to mistresses but sometimes, I get irritated when people try to make this biased comparison. I hear things like, "The mistress never complains about sex." Why will she complain? Do you know the responsibility your wife has? The mistress just remains there and has everything supplied to her by someone's husband who wouldn't mind doing the shopping for her. She doesn't have any child to look out for neither does she have responsibilities. As a matter of fact, she might even be in school and they might be on strike. I wish some men can treat their wives the same way they treat these strange women outside.

A man will not mind getting back from work and sitting down, waiting for the woman to come and serve dinner. Meanwhile, there could be food and all he needs to do is, take it out from the fridge and warm it. Yet, he would sit there to run down the wife's battery with numerous calls. One would think it is out of genuine concern without knowing that it is because he wants food and sex which is not a bad thing as a married man but at least, you should help your wife to ease the stress.

Let's treat two imaginary scenarios.

SCENARIO 1

Mrs. Jennifer works with a multinational company and is on her way back from work. She has had a busy day at work and cannot wait to rest her body at home. She even doubts if she will be able to eat; all she wants to do is to serve her husband his food, have a shower and go to bed immediately. However, she gets home and is welcomed by her husband's smiling face. He has served dinner and tells her to just freshen up so that they can eat dinner together. She giggles like a new born baby as she rushes to the bathroom to have her bath. She doesn't know when she utters the words, "I have the best husband in the world. God please bless and keep him for me." She is yet to recover from the surprise of freshly cooked dinner and she sees a handwritten note on the bed that reads, "I bless the day you decided to go on this journey called forever with me." They eat dinner while laughing and telling each other how their day went. After that, her husband makes sexual advances at her and she is so happy to give him a memorable love making session. In fact, she is so active during the session that her husband has to ask, "Is this really my wife?"

SCENARIO 2

Mrs. Omotola is a lawyer and works with the judiciary in her state of origin. She is tired from having to spend majority of her time working on a criminal case. She is just wishing to come back home and meet dinner although she knows that is merely a wishful thought. She cannot wait to prepare something light for dinner and head over to bed immediately. She gets back home and meets her husband playing games on his phone. He doesn't ask how her day was. She goes to the kitchen and asks him if she can prepare rice for dinner, at least, it won't take much time. Her husband says no and insists that he wants pounded yam. As tired as she is, she knows that refusing his request would mean war. She cooks and serves him his food. She is so tired that she skips dinner and hurries to have a bath so that she can sleep. Just when she is trying to finally fall asleep, her husband comes and demands sex. She refuses and tells him he is insensitive.

Do you see the two scenarios? No one is saying you should turn to a cook everyday but it won't be a bad idea to help out when you can. Indeed, Dr. Kevin Leman was right when he said sex begins in the kitchen.

The women in the story were both tired but the first woman did not only have sex with her husband but gave him a memorable love making session because he helped her out in some chores that made life easier for her. Don't just sit down there and watch your wife struggle alone trying to cook, do the laundry, look after the baby or children, try to complete her assignment or office work and all you do is play games on your phone while laughing so loudly at posts online. I wonder how some men do it. They are so comfortable with not helping out when they can especially when they know their wives have no housemaid. They might have been the one to kick against one. Then after the woman has stressed herself out with all the domestic work and has put the child/ children to bed and want to sleep, you start making advances and get immediately offended when she isn't giving into your advances.

For the women, you can also find out from your husband what he needs help with. Is it his laundry or feeding the dogs? This is important especially when he is working late so that he doesn't come back and have to do all those chores before joining you in bed; more so, when you know you want him.

Foreplay

This is directed mostly to the man. I understand that you might not really understand why it takes your wife a longer time to get in the mood for sex when you do nothing extraordinary to get horny almost all of the time. You need to understand that you are more moved by what you see while your wife is more moved by touch and words. You can see your wife nude and immediately want to have sex with her but for most women, it doesn't work that way. Seeing her husband naked doesn't automatically bring sexual urges for her. It is not just enough to kiss your wife for one minute and wonder why she isn't aroused. You need to study the anatomy of your wife and spend time in foreplay. It is no secret that some women find foreplay more fulfilling sexually than the actual act of sex. Don't just rush into penetration immediately. It makes your wife feel that you are only interested in satisfying yourself without taking her feelings into consideration. If you are not sure of where to touch and how to touch those places to stimulate sexual feelings, ask your wife and also watch her reaction to what you are doing.

As a wife, you also have a role to play in encouraging your husband to spend time on foreplay. Don't just stay on the bed, saying nothing. Let him know if what he is doing is pleasurable to you. If it is not, do not feel bad to tell him. Other times, you might have to teach him what to do, direct his hands to the places you want him to touch. Enough of sounding holier than God. God himself created sex and there is absolutely nothing dirty in what God created. Some feel their husbands will get angry when they tell him the truth and so they fake the moans and orgasm. That's such a high level of deception. It would leave you feeling used and that might be one of the reasons you are not excited about sex and give excuses for the sex to be postponed. Unfortunately, this is the experience of some married women. If your wife has not yet been able to achieve orgasm via penetration, she should be able to achieve that via foreplay.

Sit down as a couple and know what tickles two of you sexually. By doing this, you show that you are interested in each other's sexual life. It can be frustrating at times if your wife is a virgin and haven't understood her body yet and so you are trying your best to know what tickles her sexually but she isn't cooperating with you. I advise you keep at it and don't stop communicating. It is just a matter of time and everything will fall into place. Go for the right knowledge and implement what you have learnt.

Wives, one of the ways to encourage your husband to spend time in foreplay is to let him know that the time he spends on it is not in vain. You cannot watch him spend close to thirty minutes in foreplay with you and you still perform badly in sex. He would feel that he just wasted his time and won't be interested in doing it any longer especially when he has done that over a long period of time with no improvement. After the foreplay, wives get actively involved in sex.

Scheduled sex

This is not saying you cannot have sex anytime you want to. You are at liberty to do that as a married couple but there is this excitement scheduled sex brings. You simply set a day for it and look forward to it. For instance, the husband tells the wife we are going to make love tomorrow when we get back from church; that is scheduled sex. Both husband and wife look forward to it.

Understanding

I feel this should have come first. If we do not understand the purpose of a thing, we would likely abuse it. Understanding the purpose of anything is key, including sex. When you get to understand what sex means to your spouse, you would improve your sex life and seek help on that if need be.

What Should a Wife Understand About Her Husband's Sexual Life?

A man thinks about sex more often than you. Sex can help him boost his confidence. That's why when a man cannot maintain an erection, it affects him badly, not just sexually but he begins to see himself as a failure and this, if not handled properly, can affect his self-confidence.

Sex helps him to maintain focus at work and all he does. A man who is starved of sex can easily lose focus. When a man isn't married and has decided to stay chaste till marriage, it can be easy for him but when he is married and his wife isn't giving him sex, it can get him distracted.

For many men, sex is the deepest level of intimacy. He sees it as giving his 'all' to the woman he loves. When you constantly make excuses for sex not to take place, he interprets it differently. He might start seeing it as you not willing to help him achieve this type of intimacy he so much craves for. This might be strange to a woman's ears because the way she wants to experience intimacy is by talking and pouring her emotions to her husband who might not be willing to listen sometimes.

Sex can help a man fulfil his marriage vows of being faithful to you. Some people believe that a man that would cheat will still do so irrespective of the number of times you give him sex. Well, I do not believe that is applicable to all men as some men are willing to stay faithful to their wives as long as they are sexually satisfied. As a wife, why don't you do your part which involves satisfying his sexual needs? Do not worry if that will keep him from cheating on you or not.

What Should a Man Understand About His Wife's Sexual Needs?

Contrary to popular belief that all men do not turn down sexual advances from their wives, it would interest you to know that some men do turn down their wife's sexual advances often. It is either they are tired from work and sleep off immediately after dinner or give an excuse of headache all the time. Some men are yet to understand that their wives also need sex. It might surprise you to know that some wives have very high sex drive and it can be really frustrating to her if her husband is not willing to satisfy her sexually.

There was a woman who became a lesbian because of her husband's inability to satisfy her. She wasn't a lesbian before marriage but when she got fed up of him always coming home tired, giving excuses and always travelling for one business trip or the other, she decided to look for a way to achieve sexual pleasure and satisfaction without it raising eyebrows. Then, she settled for lesbianism.

A woman can know that she doesn't understand how to satisfy her husband sexually and seek help but most men think they know it all when their actions prove that they know nothing. Dear young husbands, it is not only your wife that is obliged to satisfy you. You are also expected to satisfy her sexually as well.

The next time you wonder why your wife is so keen about love making and thinks you are seeing someone else due to your constant refusal, understand the following:

~ She sees sex as a way to express her love for you.

~ She sees sex as a way to give and receive pleasure.

~ When she knows that she can satisfy her husband sexually, it helps to build her confidence.

Sex is a way she connects with you deeply. She knows she cannot do this with anyone else and is glad to connect with you in such a personal way. I guess this point will make you understand why women get terribly upset at a cheating husband. She cannot bring herself to understand that you are connecting this way with someone else other than her. You might see it as just sex but to her, it is more than that. Sex also produces the 'feel good' hormones in women. It makes them feel happy and fulfilled. Little wonder, people think a woman who might be getting angry always is doing that as a result of lack of sex, although that might not the reason all the time.

Here comes the commonly asked questions:

Can I turn down sexual advances from my spouse? Does it mean I have to be in the mood always?

Yes, you can turn down sexual advances from your spouse and no, you don't always have to be in the mood. What does being in the mood mean to you? You can psych yourself to get in the mood. Sex doesn't have to be abandoned until you get in the mood for it. You can initiate sex and discover that you get in the mood while in the act.

We have agreed that you can turn down sexual advances and I shall be giving diverse instances when it can be understood and permitted. However, you know your spouse better or you will know them better with time. So you can decide when you can turn down sexual advances for genuine reasons. Note that the list below is not exhaustive. Your very peculiar case might not be covered here.

ACCEPTABLE REASONS FOR TURNING DOWN YOUR SPOUSE'S SEXUAL ADVANCES AS A WIFE

— You are on your period

There are a lot of controversies on this area. Some believe that having sex during this time is dirty while others think it is not dirty. The reason people decline making love during this time might not be the dirt. They might find it very uncomfortable and afraid that it can stain their bedsheet. Do not be pressurized by an outsider to do what you don't want to do. If you and your husband have agreed not to have sex during your menstruation, then you don't have to do it. It won't be an issue since that is what you both have agreed on.

— A difficult pregnancy/Doctor's Recommendation

There was a lady that was always having miscarriages. She felt she was under demonic attack. I am not saying that it is not possible but you should also check it out medically to be sure it isn't something a small procedure can fix. After a while, she decided to seek medical help and she was informed that she needed to avoid sex for the first three months of her next pregnancy. Luckily for her, her husband was there with her to hear the doctor's advice. He was also tired of the constant miscarriages. So accepting it was easy for them.

You do not want to take chances and go against your doctor's advice especially in situations of life and death. There are other ways of achieving sexual pleasure without penetration. You can stick to those ways in such a situation.

— The Birth of a Baby

After delivery, the woman's body needs time to heal. Some people say sexual activities can resume as early as six weeks after while others say two months. However, I have heard a doctor say that one has to pay attention to her body to know when she is okay to resume her sexual duties.

The fact that your husband asks you for sex at such a time doesn't mean that you should give in. He might be doing that because he has missed making love to you. You just have to lovingly explain to him that you need just a little time to heal and you will be all his.

A lady died during the delivery of her second baby. She had her first child via Caesarean Section and was advised not to get pregnant till a year later but she got back home and resumed her sexual duties almost immediately. Unknown to the both of them, she got pregnant and it was a very tough and complicated pregnancy. Things got out of hand and she lost her life. Everyone's healing process is different. This is why most doctors recommend you pay close attention to your body. What works for one woman might not work for you.

— Extreme Fatigue

I am not talking about the usual slang of being tired that people use as an excuse to always avoid sex. If you are extremely tired and cannot have sex, lovingly inform your spouse. He/she should understand if it is not something you do often. You can still give him a warm kiss and smuggle yourself into his hands and promise to make it up to him once you get strong. Please, note that using this as a daily excuse can be irritating and frustrating for the man.

— Spiritual Exercise

This is also a valid reason to say no. According to the Bible in 1 Corinthians 7:5a, "Defraud ye not one the other, except it be with consent for a time that ye may give yourselves to fasting and prayer..."

This should be done with the consent of your partner. Inform him/her of your intention to fast. This can prepare his/her mind not to expect sex from you during the fast period. Others have argued that it is not sinful to have sex during fasting but I don't think it is right. The main reason to abstain from it during fasting isn't just because it is sinful but because you need time to concentrate and set your mind on things of the spirit. You can have sex once you break your fast in the evening.

Even if you have the right to say no due to the reasons listed above, it can be done wrongly and this can lead to further problems. The man can start having it outside or become very distant and offended because of your refusal. Some men will still be offended, distant and go out to have it irrespective of how you refuse to indulge in sex due to the reasons above but there are still good men who would be ready to wait till you come around especially if it is done in the right way. Some of the right ways of saying no includes; saying it lovingly, respectfully, looking at him with affection and with understanding.

Some Things That Can Affect Your Sex Life Negatively

Some things that can affect a woman's sex life negatively include the following:

— **A negative self-image**

You do not see yourself attractive enough to stand naked before your husband. You might even be wondering what your husband saw in you due to the negative self-image you have. You should know that your husband saw other women; probably more physically attractive than you but still settled for you. This knowledge should help you develop a positive self-image. It doesn't matter if your mother told you how she almost aborted you at birth or if you were always the ugly and odd one among your friends or if you couldn't attract guys to yourself in the past. You need to know that beauty is more than the physical attributes.

— Being uncomfortable with your body

A lot of wives are very uncomfortable in their bodies. They feel God made a mistake when creating some of their body parts. They hate their small breasts, flat buttocks, unattractive hips, big tummy; so you switch to defensive mood anytime your husband suggests a sexual style that could make these attributes more obvious to your husband. You are only comfortable with styles that hide those attributes that you term unattractive. What if I tell you that your husband might not even notice them or even if he does, he might not see it as a big deal? A lady said she had a scar on her breast and when she newly got married, she was uncomfortable with that scar. She was secretly praying it disappears while she continuously told her husband how much she hated the scar. One day, he said to her, "I don't know why you are making such a big deal out of this scar. I don't even see it that way. I have no issue with it." You can imagine that she was just giving herself needless worry and letting it make her uncomfortable about her body. A lot of wives do not want the lights on during sexual activities, not because they hate light at night, which is perfectly normal for some but because they don't want their body to be seen.

They also hide in the bathroom to dress up. Once you are uncomfortable with your body, it will influence your sex life negatively.

— Health Issues

It is worthy of note that some wives might want to step up their sex game but cannot do that because of health issues. Do not hesitate to see a doctor when you feel something is wrong in your body. It could be an hormonal imbalance issue that needs medical attention or something more serious. One who is seriously sick cannot participate fully in love making.

— Resentment About Your Husband

It's possible he did something to you in the past and has apologized but you are yet to forgive him or you have suddenly developed resentment towards him. You cannot understand why there is no love like before. You need to fix this as early as you can because it can affect your sex life negatively. Have you noticed that it is easier to warm up towards your husband when you are happy with him? It is the same thing here. When you feel resentment towards him, you are bound to avoid getting intimate with him. You would want to avoid him like a plague. Even his attempt to touch you can make you feel very irritated and uncomfortable. Work on this as fast as possible. If it means talking to a marriage counsellor, do so.

— Fear of Pregnancy

You must have just given birth and you do not want to get pregnant immediately or you do not mind getting pregnant immediately but are afraid of the implications as you have been told to wait for a while and so you are so afraid of sex. You need to discuss this fear with your husband and see a health practitioner together that can help you choose a comfortable family planning method out of the numerous ones that exist. You cannot say you won't have sex again until you want your next baby. Sweetheart, sex is not only for procreation; it is also for pleasure.

— You Dread Contacting Sexually Transmitted Diseases

That is why it is important to discuss openly with your husband. Husbands, I sincerely hope you get to read this book with your wife. You cannot afford to sleep with anyone apart from your wife. It has a way of making her run away from sex. If your husband was unfaithful in the past and you haven't been able to have sexual intercourse with him, even if you have forgiven him as you're now concerned about your health, it is high time you had a heart to heart discussion with him. If he needs to be tested for all sexually transmitted diseases and certified clean, encourage him to do it.

— Hectic Schedules

You probably just got a new job, a promotion at work or you are still at your old place of work but it was easier when you weren't married and now you are married and not willing to let go of your job, you do not know how to cope as you are always overwhelmed with hectic work and tight schedules. You need to look for a way to balance things up. Don't allow your marriage, especially your sex life, suffer as a result of this. You haven't had sex with your husband in two months because of your tight schedule at work and you seem comfortable about it. You admit he claims to love you and should understand, he is a pastor and cannot cheat on you, and the money you're making is helping the family. You are right but if you also love him, you would care about his needs. It is a different ball game if you are out of town and cannot fulfil this need. The fact that he is a pastor doesn't mean he doesn't have sexual feelings; he is also a man. The money you make cannot fill the vacuum that lack of sex creates. It is true that he might be understanding but for how long do you want him to continue understanding? If the tables were turned, would you like it?

Always look for ways to quickly balance things up because this can negatively affect your sex life.

— He Is Boring in Bed

Women are not the only ones that can be boring in bed. Some men are also boring in bed and know nothing about how to please a woman. The sad thing is that very few of them are ready to seek help. They feel it is a slap on their manhood. If your husband falls under this category, you need to encourage him to seek help. It won't be a bad idea if you teach him. These days, there are good sex coaches and learning these things can be done from the comfort of your home as there are mostly online classes. Encourage him good books. If your husband is not satisfying you in bed, you won't get excited about love making and this will affect your sex life negatively.

I know that some men might still read this section even if I am particularly addressing the women. Ask your wife how she feels about your love making skills. Don't proudly think the way you make love to her is the best thing that has happened to the human race after the birth of our Lord Jesus Christ. If she tells you she has never enjoyed any love making session with you, you should be bothered and look for ways to fix it. If you release too soon, seek help and don't make the mistake of thinking it is absolutely normal and the same with every other man.

— Trying to Conceive

Doctors, family members and everyone that mean well for you or not keep telling you to make love often. You have been following their advice religiously, yet, pregnancy has not occurred. It is easy for those who haven't gone through this phase to try to take your feelings lightly. You might even hear things like, "Enjoy your sex life now. Once children come, you will be so bothered about not getting pregnant." You are tempted to start thinking that you are wasting your time since the sex isn't fulfilling the outcome you so desire at the moment which is pregnancy but you have to get over that feeling. We are all humans and once in a while, the thought might come up. Knowing what to do with the thought is more important than the thought itself. Tell yourself that you are making love with your husband because he is your husband. Sex was also designed for pleasure and other benefits.

You can talk to those who experienced delay and are now parents to find out how they kept their sex life active despite the delay. Luckily enough, people are not ashamed to share their experiences these days. You can also surf the net, join a community of like-minded people, read and listen to how they spiced up their sex life. At the end of the day, know that you still need to have sex to get pregnant.

A lady shared her experience of how delay in conception affected her sex life with her husband. She was so irritated each time he asked for sex; more like, what have the ones we've been having yielded? Her husband kept encouraging her that she has to stop thinking that sex is only for baby making and give herself the permission to enjoy her sex life as this was negatively affecting it. It took her time to do that but after she did that, she started relaxing more during their love making sessions and it wasn't long before she found out that she was pregnant.

Let no one deceive you. If you do not take control of your feeling and emotions during the period you are actively trying to conceive with no positive outcome, it can affect your sex life negatively.

— Certain Medications

Some medications can affect our sex life negatively. It is no fault of yours that you're probably on certain medications but once you find out that your sex drive has reduced drastically, reach out to your doctor or health provider and find out if this is caused by the drug/drugs they administered to you. This is why I always advise people to read through the pamphlets of drugs. Be sure you can cope with the side effects and if your suspicions are right, lovingly inform your husband and ask your doctor if something can be done to reduce the side effect of the drugs.

— Pressure to Be What You Aren't

If you're pressurized by your husband to be sexier in bed and act like a movie star and you are upset wishing you can tell him how that expectation is affecting your sex life negatively, simply tell him his high expectations are making you nervous. You don't have to wish for something you can easily have or do. Tell him you will improve if he wants you to but constantly comparing you to the ladies he has been with in the past or pressurizing you affects your sex life negatively.

— Dealing with Mental Issues

We tend to shy away from this topic but that doesn't mean it is not happening to our mothers, sisters and wives. If you notice you are always depressed and anxious in such a way that it has affected your sex life negatively, you need to seek help. Some depressed people resort to drinking alcohol to stupor. Be reminded that this can affect your sex life negatively.

— Seeing Sex as A Tool

When you see sex as something you give when you are happy and in talking terms with your husband and something you withhold when he has offended you, it can affect your sex life negatively as you will definitely withhold it when he offends you or when he hasn't met your expectations. Seeing sex as a tool is a wrong mentality. See it as one of the responsibilities that marriage bestows on you.

As a wife, you can have a positive view of sex and be willing to enjoy sexual pleasure with your husband but he might not be interested. It might have nothing to do with him having an affair with any other woman. The same can also apply for the man.

Below are few reasons your spouse might be uninterested in sex even when all other things we have discussed above seem to be taken care of.

— Body Odour

Your body smells badly that your spouse prefers to sleep or go without sex for days or months than come close to you. The bad thing is when you have an incorrigible spouse; one that cannot be corrected. You might have told your spouse in time past that their body is smelling and request that they have a bath but they took it as an insult and created a scene out of it. He/ she might have said, "Is it only my body that smells?" There are some people like that.

Pay attention to your body. You cannot go out, work the whole day, get back home totally exhausted sweating profusely and you don't want to take a bath. It can be tolerated if you two couldn't just wait for that and had sex in the heat of passion but going to the bed that way and expecting your spouse to make love to you is a no-no. This is not only because of sex; you should be concerned about your personal hygiene as well. Don't carry your mouth that smells of onions, 'suya' and the last meal you ate to kiss your wife. Some wives cannot pretend and will immediately say something you might not like. Freshen up and be clean.

You can't expect your spouse to engage in oral sex and you are refusing to wash up. You should wash up and if you want it more engaging, you can ask your spouse to help you wash your private part. This can even be a form of foreplay.

It isn't a crime to use deodorant on your armpit and wear an inviting night wear. If you decide to be nude, it's fine but make sure your body isn't smelling. I wish there is a nicer word to be used but I found none. We must tell ourselves the truth. Some of us automatically become very conscious of our appearance when we have guests that are spending the night in our home but care less once they leave. That's wrong.

— Nagging Attitude

There is a huge difference between telling your partner how you feel and nagging. Let me speak to the wives; somehow, we have been taught to believe that our husbands can do 'anything' for us when in that mood of sex. However, when it becomes a continuous thing, it sends the wrong signal to the man. Must it be when you have to satisfy your husband sexually that you suddenly remember the human hair he hasn't bought for you or the cash he promised? You won't just stop at remembering it in your mind but you suddenly voice out and start complaining nonstop. Most men would suddenly lose their erection regardless of how hard it was.

— Dirty Room

The whole place looks stuffy, unkempt and dirty. The bed sheets haven't been changed in months. A side of the bed sheet is stained with menstrual blood from your last month's cycle. Another side is stained with brown powder while the ground is so dirty that one cannot help but wonder if a container of sand was emptied there. I know that we are all busy with work, business and our personal life but we should be very conscious of how our house looks especially our bedroom. This is the place we retire to at the end of every day.

— Breast Milk Stain

Congratulations on being a mother. It is a beautiful experience for those that are first time moms. However, your body should not always smell of breast milk and even if it does, once you know it is time for sexual intercourse, try and freshen up. Your husband might not like the stain of breast milk all over your night gown.

— Business/Work Issues

It is possible that your husband has issues at work. For instance, he lost his boss at work or a huge sum of money due to a wrong business transaction that can make him lose interest in everything around him; sex inclusive. It is worse when he has pressing financial needs and has no one to run to.

— Difficulty in Getting an Erection

Your husband might suddenly find out that he can't get an erection. It could be surprising to him and as such, he doesn't know how to tell you about it yet. He might be secretly seeking a solution to it and anytime you try to initiate sex, he might become defensive trying to give one excuse or the other. If this is the case, dear young husband, you need to open up to your wife and seek immediate help. Wives, please take it easy. No matter how much you think it is affecting you, also bear in mind that it is affecting him. This is a time to seek immediate help.

— Personal Reasons

Your spouse might be going through personal stuff that they are not ready to talk about or do not know how to go about. They might have gotten news from home and want it to remain within their family of orientation for the time being. Your wife might have been threatened by her boss at work who is trying to make advances at her. She might be thinking of quitting her job as a result of this but she is scared and wondering if she is actually ready to be a housewife or if she would be able to get another job soon. It is also possible that it might have nothing to do with your spouse but a friend. Her best friend might have confided in her that she caught her husband with another woman and she is still surprised, trying to assimilate the bad news; maybe this is a man she looked up to and felt he had strong moral values. She could be shocked. This kind of feeling at that time can affect her negatively and even if everything is perfect for love making, she won't be ready for it.

— **You Seem to Be Distant**

You don't say no to an invitation for sexual intercourse but you seem to be absent while in the act. It feels like rape. You are lost in thoughts such that you don't respond to what your partner is saying during sex; not because you don't want to respond but because you did not hear what your spouse said. This can be tolerated if it is not a regular occurrence but when it becomes a regular occurrence, one is forced to avoid sexual intercourse so that you don't look distant again. This is worse if it only happens during sexual intercourse. One can easily read meaning to it especially when your spouse asks you what the issue is and you say nothing.

— **Not Participating in Sex**

You are passive in the act of love making. Dear young wife, I don't know about your husband but most young men love their wives being actively involved in the act. Why lay there like a log of wood when you can move? You make it look like a hell of work every time he tries to turn you to change position. You don't mind slapping him or telling him how ungodly those positions are. Who said they are ungodly? Even God loves varieties and that's why he created different colours and shapes, height and languages etc.

A man who is not fully grounded in God can be funny with his sex life. I guess you have heard some men say they cannot eat the same soup everyday when asked why they can't stay faithful to one person. You need to be willing to participate and keep the bed hot with varieties of sexual styles. Let your husband not be able to guess what you will bring up during the next sexual act. The same applies to the men. Even if you got married as a virgin, learn to spice things up.

— **A Hungry Spouse**

As funny as this might sound, this can actually be a reason for your spouse to turn down sex. Relax! Don't think it always has to be an affair or something big or bad. Do you remember how you feel when you haven't eaten for long hours and you are hungry? Some of us snap at everyone and everything around us.

A man was very hungry as he had not eaten for two days and he finally had the opportunity to eat. He decided to set his whole barn on fire, thinking that he would finish all the yams there because of how hungry he was but he ate just a portion of one tuber of yam and was satisfied. When your spouse has had a long day at work and they specifically tell you that they are hungry, allow them to eat. The sex will not go sour. Is sex work? Yes, sex is work but a good type of work. It is also an exercise and if people feel tired after an exercise, then it is normal for people to feel tired after sex especially if it was a sexual experience of many rounds. Your spouse knowing the kind of energy they exert during sex might not want to engage in it if they haven't eaten.

— Trying to Get Your Attention

Your spouse might have known that the only time you are willing to listen to what they have to say is when they refuse your sexual advances. So they refuse it in order to have your attention. It is very wrong but that shows what some people place more value on; you can be talking about how your day went, your trip to your children's school, what your parents said and he is so busy on his phone, playing games. Many men are fond of this. He won't notice when you leave him but try to say no to his advances and he would be ready to listen to you and know your reason.

Be that as it may, it could be a good time to get his attention and tell him all you have to say before getting down to the act but you need to address this issue so that it doesn't get out of hand or become a norm.

— Painful Sex

There are different reasons for pain during intercourse. If you are a virgin, you might need to use a lubricant during your honeymoon; reason being that most virgins might not still get wet after foreplay as they are yet to understand their body and what tickles them sexually. Instead of depriving your partner of sex, get a good lubricant and don't worry about it killing the little swimmers. There are sperm friendly lubricants.

If you are confused about the painful sex you keep having, it could be due to different reasons. I can't pin-point anyone. I suggest you see a doctor.

BEST SEXUAL POSITION

I researched this and was ready to write my findings but I suddenly had an inspiration to leave this open to the couples involved. I cannot tell people the best sexual position to practice. It is left for them to discover that on their own. What one couple sees as the best style that gives them multiple orgasms might not work for another couple.

If it's a new marriage, don't be discouraged. Take it easy on yourselves while exploring the hundreds of sexual positions and I'm sure that in no distant time, you would discover the style that is best for you and your spouse. Should you need help on specific sexual need or counselling, do not be ashamed to see a professional. I run one-on-one consulting sessions for new couples. You can always book a slot for a full conversation. Sex is a beautiful gift created by God. It has to be enjoyed.

Love Birds Exercise 6.

• Have your spouse been complaining of the way you make love to him/her? If yes, are you willing to adjust in areas that need your adjustment?

• As a wife, do you feel you need your husband to spend more time on foreplay? If yes, encourage him to do that following the steps suggested in this chapter.

• As a couple, discuss what sex means to the both of you and genuinely point out areas that need improvement?

• If you have been uninterested in making love lately, tell your spouse the genuine reason/reasons for that?

• What new thing would you try sexually in bed?

CHAPTER SEVEN

REACHING OUT FOR HELP

There is a wrong notion about reaching out for help. Some people make marriage look like a cult and frown at couples who discuss their marital issues with people. I do not support talking about the issues in your marriage to just anyone as a lot of people cannot offer you any help. They just want to know what is going on in your home and laugh but there is an exception to this. There are some people that are professionally trained to guide you through the hurdles in your marriage.

Of course, God is the ultimate help but God has given marriage counsellors the wisdom to help marriages experiencing turbulent times. It's about locating the right person; one that can hold your hands through it all and offer you godly counsel. It is like saying we should not go to school because we have God or we shouldn't go to the hospital at all.

A lot of young couples are secretly dying in silence and are afraid to tell anyone. They have been trained to believe that you must not speak out. Speaking out does not mean you are running down your marriage or your spouse. Most times, you might be the one that needs help, not your spouse and so in reality, you aren't reporting your spouse but looking for ways to get help for the good of your spouse and marriage in the long run.

I remember when I also needed help on a particular aspect of my marriage when I just got married. My husband was excited when he started seeing the positive results of that counselling I got from a woman I love and respect so much who has been married for close to 20 years.

Dear young couple, don't listen to those who tell you that everybody's marriage is bitter and going through serious issues. I get surprised when I hear people say marriage is a scam and that no one is enjoying their marriage. Some people are actually enjoying their marriages and are so happy together that their children are blessed to have them as parents and also know what to look for in their future spouse. You and your spouse might be meant to be together and the constant disagreements you are having could be as a result of lack of understanding or little issues that can be fixed if you decide to seek help. Marriage counsellors and mentors know that they have to keep the confidentiality of their clients.

I do not mean that you should run to a counsellor over every little problem. There are some issues that can be handled on your own without involving anyone. Wisdom can help you avoid some issues. For example, as the husband, you like pressing toothpaste from the top and your wife prefers pressing it from the bottom; this is an issue that can be handled with wisdom. Simply get two toothpaste tubes if the other person is not set to adjust.

There are some areas that you need to seek immediate help when going through. If not, they can have a strain on your health and well-being to the point that you don't enjoy your marriage. It is worse when the issue is left unattended to until it starts affecting your mental health. The serious problems related to mental health are often overlooked probably because of the stereotype surrounding it and the fear of being seen or perceived as a retarded person when that might not be the case.

Below are areas you must seek godly counsel:

— **Abuse of Any Form**

Your spouse suddenly becomes aggressive and abuses you constantly. Abuse is abuse; be it emotional, physical and verbal. You keep getting hit by your husband at the slightest provocation. You are trying very hard to hold on or you keep believing that things will get better but everything keeps getting worse. Your face has been disfigured because of the constant beatings and everyone who is close to you knows that something is wrong. You are so withdrawn and you prevent your parents and siblings from visiting. They might have warned you against marrying your husband due to his anger issues but you still went ahead and felt love and marriage will change it and here you are, practically turned to a punching bag.

You keep telling people that you fell down and that's the reason for your swollen eyes and black circle underneath your eyes but you know that isn't true. Your last miscarriage came as a shock to your doctor because at the time of your last scan during your ante-natal care, everything was fine. Your doctor keeps insisting that the miscarriage isn't normal and wants to know more but you keep telling him you fell down and you get angry that he wants to know everything.

You have been told by your husband to cut off from everyone. That's usually the tactics of abusers. They make it feel like you need only them, they love you more than others and if you dare to leave, you would be totally helpless without them.

Darling, I am not telling you to leave but you need to seek help quickly. Don't remain there and die in silence. Do you want to wait till they carry your corpse out of that marriage? You might have been so traumatized to the point that you feel suicide or death is the best option to escape the pain. Sweetheart, you aren't useless at all. Even if you feel you are no longer useful to yourself, think about your parents, siblings and friends who genuinely love you. How would they feel if that happens to you?

You might also be concerned about what people will say; maybe you have children already and do not want them to grow up without you or you do not have the means to take care of them yourself or you see marriage as your greatest achievement in life. That's okay. I am not suggesting that you leave your marriage immediately. I am only suggesting you seek help. Your husband might also be willing to change but doesn't know how to go about it. He feels bad and cries every time he hits you or you have gotten so used to the beatings that you now look forward to it.

Fine, you should be praying for your husband but while you are praying, seek help. He may need to see a counsellor, psychologist, or emotional therapist. You might also need to see the above set of people. Your mentality might have been set to believe that it is normal or that love must be expressed in such a way but you are wrong. Love doesn't hurt. A thorough study of all the characteristics of love listed in the Bible (1 Corinthians 13:4-7) reveals that none talked of beatings.

For some wives, they are not abused physically but verbally and emotionally. Your husband keeps reminding you that he married you because you were pregnant and he didn't want to have a child outside wedlock. He could be accusing you of obstructing his once planned life. He tells you how useless you are, eating his money and getting fat. What about those that have lost their self-esteem because of emotional and verbal abuse? I won't forget a man who kept abusing his wife verbally because she took in before the wedding and he had to hurry the wedding. As far as I am concerned, even if that act is wrong, she didn't get herself pregnant. Two of them were in the act together. The day the woman threatened to leave the marriage, he started begging like a child. It left me wondering if he was doing that to make the woman feel he did her a favour by getting married to her or if he was doing it to keep her under mental bondage. I wish I knew the answers to those questions but I don't.

I find it ridiculous when people regard verbal abuse as nothing. We can't treat such an ill as nothing. In 2018, while everyone was getting ready to enjoy the Christmas holiday, the Internet carried the story of a young lady with a promising future that took her life because her mother kept using hurtful words on her. She tried her best to get the love, affection and care of her mother and it wasn't working. One fateful day, she decided to take her own life.

I have always maintained that emotional wounds are more dangerous as they can't be seen by the doctors and given immediate attention. Most times, before the person notices it and decides to give it attention, it is already late. The strange behaviour of most married men and women is as a result of these emotional wounds they've had since childhood and kept to themselves.

Some husbands also experience physical, emotional and verbal abuse from their wives. This might sound strange but there are some husbands that are constantly beaten by their wives. What about wives that abuse their husbands anywhere with no iota of respect? I only used the example of wives going through such experiences because the percentage is more than that of the husbands.

Always reach out for help if you find yourself in such a situation.

— Depression and Suicidal Thoughts

The way we react to situations around us is different and unique to us. Two people might be going through the same situation and it could be more overwhelming on one of them than the other. Even identical twins can have the same facial attributes which make it almost impossible to differentiate one from the other especially if you didn't grow up with them or haven't known them for a long time but that doesn't mean that they will behave exactly the same way.

That's the same thing with marriage, two people might be going through the exact thing and react differently. The impact of what they are going through will be totally different. You know yourself better and the effect your husband's abuse is having on you. If you are always depressed and having suicidal thoughts, please reach out for help immediately. Don't allow someone who might be enjoying her own issues prevent you from seeking help. Remember you both are not the same. Your friend facing the same challenge might have grown up in a family where her father was beating her mother always and as such, she sees it as the normal way of life. She might have dated guys in the past who beat her and she was totally okay with it or she might see it as a way to express love.

On the other hand, you grew up in a family where you saw your parents hug and play together joyfully. Your last relationship before you met your husband ended because the man tried hitting you. Are you seeing that the two of you are not the same? Don't make anyone your yardstick for reaching out for professional help.

Issue with Anger Management

Anger in itself isn't a sin as it is simply a reaction towards something we term unpleasant. However, allowing your anger to get out of hand becomes a serious issue.

"Be ye angry, and sin not; let not the sun go down upon your wrath."

Ephesians 4:26

While I was writing this book, I woke up one beautiful morning and didn't see my husband in bed. I knew he was listening to the early morning news in the living room. I went to the parlour and met him listening to news just as I predicted. He kept looking at his phone and said, "Baby, come and see." I went and he showed me the video his friend sent to him through WhatsApp. It was about a man who shot his wife and two sons as a result of anger; the police asked him to give his statement. He said his wife kept accusing him of having an extra-marital affair as he comes back home late most times. On one of those days he got back from work, he barely spent time at home and was about going out again. The wife got angry and accused him of having a secret affair at odd hours. He ignored her and still went out. When he got back home, he noticed that his wife and two sons were sleeping in the room and the door was locked. He called her to open the door but she sensed that he was sounding angry and was scared to open it. He got angrier, brought his gun and fired it through the door. That killed her and their two sons who were on the bed. The sad thing was that they had been married for ten years and were blessed with three children.

I was so cold throughout that day. Of course, he was arrested but that didn't bring back his wife and two children. The twenty-eight year old lady was cut off in her prime. This is a serious issue that shouldn't be overlooked in homes. When you notice that you get so angry and don't mind breaking everything in the house and being violent, seek help. If you have a violent spouse, encourage him/her to also seek help.

I've heard of men that lock their wives up and beat them mercilessly. What usually saves them are neighbours who hear their cry and run to help. What happens when your neighbours aren't around? What happens when you start staying alone in a compound without neighbours? Marriage is not a cult. What's the fate of the young lady that lost her life and two children? She's dead and gone. If we can keep getting updates about her husband, it won't be long and he would be a free man. Can you guess what people would advise? "Forgive yourself, don't you think you should get married again? Your wife is gone for life."

Strong Hatred/Resentment for Your Spouse

You are suddenly finding yourself filled with hatred and rage for your spouse. Your husband or wife might have cheated or done something wrong and because of that, you are filled with strong resentment towards him/her. We tend to act as if all is well when deep down, we know that things are not as well as we paint them. Your husband might have cheated on you and you are yet to forgive him. It could be that you found out in the most despicable manner and he is not ready to apologise. Family and friends you have confided in do not make things better. They tell you not to talk about it with him. They ask you to act nice, dress seductively, pray more, be more submissive, respect him; after all he is taking care of you.

I seriously do not know how we got here but I'm certain it is not a good place. What makes you think every husband that has ever cheated on his wife did so because his wife failed in being a good wife? It is high time we stopped that. We have to stop trivializing cheating and unfaithfulness in all its forms.

It is a completely different thing when a man cheats and is deeply sorry and tries to make amends but when he acts like it's his right, it's terrible. Some go as far as cheating with their house help, wife's relative, secretary at the office and try to justify it. Most often than not, the wife of such a husband can develop strong hatred and resentment towards the man.

If this is not well managed, it can lead to something dangerous. You need to seek help and speak to someone who truly understands, not one that will just wave it aside as if it is normal and appropriate. It is very dangerous to remain in that state because another wrong move from the man can make you snap and do what you would spend the rest of your life regretting and paying the consequences for.

In 2017, the Internet was filled with pictures of a lawyer who cut off the genitals of her husband and watched him bleed to death. It was more surprising that she was a lawyer and obviously knew the law too well and the consequences of her action. So what happened? She got really irritated and didn't know when it got out of hand. I heard they were sleeping at night and she got up and did that. Before he could fight for his life, it was too late. It was reported that the man was having an affair. The easiest thing people always advise is leaving the marriage. They say it as if it is as easy as ABC. The woman would be analysing so many things including the sacrifices, years and time she has put into the marriage. I don't support murder and that is why I am advising you seek help.

What about the husband? Your wife must have been raped in your presence and you suddenly do not want to see her. You aren't blaming her for the incident but you also cannot get over it; you are irritated by her sight. Each time you see her, all you remember is how those thieves took turns on her. This incident has turned you to a drunkard and caused you to start keeping late nights. I suggest you find someone who has been trained professionally to handle such issues and pour out your heart to the person.

You can't keep tormenting your wife in such a way as she too might be grieving privately and trying to be strong. There is a healing power in pouring out your mind to someone who truly understands. You just feel light and empty; remember the emphasis is on a person who truly understands.

Series of Miscarriages

We tend to avoid talking about this aspect probably because it is a very sensitive issue and quite personal. Pregnant women have this special bond with their babies once they find out that they are pregnant. It is a joyful moment for almost every women especially when they are married and eagerly looking forward to the time that they will become parents. Having one miscarriage is not easy. When it becomes a regular occurrence, it's worse. So they are afraid of getting pregnant again for the fear of another miscarriage. When a woman loses her pregnancy for a first time, she consoles herself that she will get pregnant again. She might be right. She gets pregnant again but it keeps ending up in a miscarriage over again. Imagine someone having over twenty miscarriages in a short while. Such a person needs urgent help. When her in-laws do not care about what she is going through, she can cope if her husband is there for her but what happens when he isn't? He might want to be there but his work makes that quite difficult. This can make someone who isn't conscious of her mental health go into despair. She starts feeling she is useless just because she can't carry a baby to full term yet.

The doctors might be doing all they can to help her and giving explanations for that but all those explanations do not change the fact that she is having series of miscarriages. She needs to keep her mind sound. Most times, people who go through this do not feel comfortable opening up to people they know. It's not because they don't trust or love them; they do but are afraid of the way they might be viewed. People tend to see everything in a negative light. She might have confided in someone before and it became the talk of town. So she knows she can't tell the same person again.

It is normal to grieve but as soon as you find out you are not getting better or you are losing the zeal to live or you don't mind resigning from your job or you don't want to stay around anyone, talk to someone. Sometimes, these issues could have nothing to do with you or your past. We live in a world where people always want to attach miscarriage to numerous abortions that might not be the case.

You know the effect the miscarriages are having on you. Do not wait until you lose your mind or the issue gets out of hand. Reach out for help.

No Communication

You and your spouse are not communicating like before. You are trying your best but your spouse is not interested. You just know that this is not normal. We are all created as social beings and that's why God didn't just create us and leave us alone. He placed us in families. While it is true that other factors might be responsible for this (stress at work, new responsibilities), you should have known the person you got married to and when it is beyond those things. He is not communicating with you but very busy chatting with total strangers online. He is not ready to talk with you for even a minute but speaks on phone for hours, laughing and smiling in between. You ask, "How was work, honey?" and he screams, "Fine!" meanwhile he was someone who could explain how work was in details. This isn't about his workload at the office or the way he is. You just know something is wrong.

Your wife isn't ready to tell you anything. Before now, she could talk for hours but not anymore. It's not as if she is tired or stressed up but each time you try to find out the reason for that, she waves it aside. You notice that she is always happy to leave the house and speak with a particular person. Don't bottle it up. This could be a warning sign and it might be something that can be redeemed if given adequate attention early enough. It would be dangerous for couples to ignore it and say, "If that is how we are going to be from now on, I am fine with it."

There was a man who noticed that his jovial and happy wife was now withdrawn and there was no form of communication between them. He ignored it and later, he found out his wife was having an affair with someone else. The day he went through their chats, he almost fainted. Nature doesn't give room for vacuum. If you both are not communicating effectively with each other and there is no known and explained reason for that, you both have found someone else to share your day's activities with, your happy and down moment. It could start as a harmless act but if care is not taken, it might degenerate into something else.

Don't wait until it gets out of hand. When you notice that the communication isn't like before and there is no known reason for that and you have also tried to find out the reason but the other person isn't ready to talk about it, you need to reach out for help.

Your partner might not be willing to communicate with you because you've hurt him/her and you are not aware. When you see a counselor and pour out your heart, you will be shocked at the things your spouse says are the reasons for the coldness and unwillingness to communicate.

One or Both of You Had an Affair

Some affairs are planned and well executed and some people do not care if they are caught or not but some others who fell into sexual sins did not plan it at all. They just got so close to someone and the person ended up taking advantage of them during their vulnerable period. This is one of the reason I advise people to be careful about who they tell their marital issues to. The Internet is not a place to post your problems openly or anything that could make someone know that you and your spouse are having issues. Once you post online, "Women cannot be trusted. I wonder how I got myself in this trap called marriage", some ladies who have been secretly admiring you would start sending private messages to you. Some of them could be worse than your wife but will pretend to be good to get your attention. Since you are in a vulnerable state, you might pour out your heart to your new friend or secretary and in no time, the deed is done. Two things are likely to happen after this; either you feel bad, apologize to your wife and promise never to do it again or you keep quiet, go back and continue doing it, after all, no one knows and you think you cannot be caught in the act.

The first option won't be easy because it can lead to more issues in your home initially but you need to do it if you are really sorry about what you have done. The fact that you told your wife doesn't mean she would forgive you immediately, thank you and cook your favourite meal for being truthful. In fact, depending on the person you cheated on her with, it might take her time to get over it. She might become distant and unwillingly to forgive. On the other hand, she might forgive you but the trust would be totally gone. You need to seek help from a professional.

It is also possible that while you are confessing your sins to your wife, she also tells you she was unfaithful; she sees it as the perfect time to open up too.

I heard of a man who was promiscuous. Each time his wife talked about it in her little way, he wouldn't listen. Sometimes, he would argue when caught in the act. After a while, she stopped talking and somehow started having an affair. He was happy thinking his wife is finally allowing him breathe. She was always happy each time he left the house and didn't care if he got back home late until he suspected this new attitude of his wife one day and decided to lie that he was going out of town for a business meeting. The wife volunteered to pack his cloths and take him to the airport.

He declined and said his friend would do that. He just hanged around his office and got back late at night. He had his own house keys. So he opened the door and went inside the house but noticed that another man's cloths were littered everywhere. Let me spare you all the nasty part. In summary, he caught his wife with another man.

Of course, it was devastating to him. It took them time to decide if they still wanted to be together. Some men would have said, "It is over. How dare you cheat on me?" but he knew he was also guilty and couldn't apportion blames. They got through that terrible phase of their marriage by seeking the needed help. Was it easy? No, it wasn't but they knew what they wanted and cleared their schedule to include weekly therapy and counselling as they asked the Holy Spirit for help together. Today, it is hard to know that such a thing happened except they tell you.

Shocking Discoveries

Married couples are often encouraged not to hide things from each other but this is not usually the case for everyone. Sometimes, that isn't their real intention. They only do that for the fear of losing the other person. I do not support this because when the other person finds out eventually, it can destroy the trust in the marriage and shake the very foundation of their marriage. Some men had children before marriage and kept shut. Women also hide terrible things from their husbands. For instance, a woman had an abortion in the past and it affected her reproductive organs. She knows it but decides to keep quiet about it. I am not saying she has to tell her husband the number of men she has slept with in the past but this is a very delicate issue. They might have been trying to have a child for some time and she is suspecting that is the reason but has decided to keep quiet about it. Her doctor might be aware of it and one day, he mistakenly tells her husband thinking that he knows about it.

It can be difficult for the man to forgive his wife in this situation, not because the abortion she did in the past affected her reproductive organ, but because she hid such a vital thing from him. She might have gotten pregnant as a result of rape but this is not a secret that has effect on only her. It also has an effect on the ability of her husband to become a father. God is the giver of children and has the final say but your husband deserves to know.

Imagine him finding out from the test results you locked up in your box and maybe you took them out to pray and forgot to return them. Then, he comes home unannounced to meet them.

What about the husband? Your wife might have seen a boy that resembles you on the day you both got married. It's possible that she noticed the striking resemblance and asked if he was your son but you laughed over it, telling her he is your sister's child she had for a man who ran away. You must have painted the story in such a way that she tells you she doesn't mind being a second mother to the young lad only for her to find out later that the boy is your biological son and the lady you described as your sister is the boy's mother. This discovery can break the marriage if not handled properly.

At this point, there is no need to pretend that all is well when you know that you two are living like total strangers in the house. Your wife is crying for feeling betrayed. She is angrier with your family members and wonders why no one told her. She might begin to wonder why the boy's mother attended her wedding and if she is safe. So many thoughts and questions that only you can answer are bound to run through her mind. She doubts you can ever tell the truth if you could be bold enough to hide such an issue and call your own biological son, your nephew.

You might have found out that your husband is gay or your wife is a lesbian. These discoveries are not easy to deal with. You might be confused on the next step to take. Going through this alone won't be easy. Firstly, you could be afraid to confide in your family members or spiritual leaders as this area is still being seen as something people do not want to talk about. You are also afraid of what would happen to your spouse if the government finds out. You can't wrap your thoughts around it. It's worse if you had a feeling about that but pushed it aside. He must have looked at your brother with admiration such that you couldn't help but ask yourself why he stared lustfully at a fellow man. She might have touched your sister inappropriately or your sister must have tried reporting to you that your wife stares make her feel naked and uncomfortable but you pushed it aside and thought she doesn't like your wife or it is the normal jealousy that do exist among ladies.

It will not be an easy journey but you two have to start by saying everything that the other person has to know no matter how difficult it is. Most times, the other person that has been betrayed might need closure. They don't necessarily want a divorce but they want time to figure some things out and heal. At this time, you should not be thinking of what anyone would say. If you need to see a marriage counsellor together with your spouse, do so. If you aren't comfortable with telling anyone apart from your spouse about it, you don't have to tell any other person.

Staying Together Just Because of the Children

In few years of being married, you are already regretting the marriage. The only reason you are still there is your children. You are not hiding it from your spouse. You keep telling your spouse that you're there because of the kids. You're saying you would have left the marriage if you didn't have children. Sincerely, you need to seek help as soon as possible. What happens when the children leave? The danger in this is that you would start seeing your kids as obstacles to your freedom. You should be able to love your spouse for who they are.

Some send their children to boarding schools at a very tender age. So what happens when they leave for school? Would two of you live like cat and dog in the house until your children return? Do you know that children of these days are smart? The child might start exhibiting traits of distress and find it difficult to concentrate in school. At home, the child/ children would be crying every time they see both of you fighting and cursing each other.

The moment you start feeling that you are remaining in a marriage because of your children, know that there is an issue. Marriage was first of all created for companionship before procreation. It is not a time to deny your feelings or feel it is normal. It is actually abnormal. I have a woman I greatly respect and I can vividly remember that she went for the last holiday with just her husband. I jokingly asked her, "Ma, what about the children?" She said they were with their grandmother and that she needed some alone time with her husband. I could sense love and excitement in her voice. That's the way it should be. You two were together before the child/children came and will still be together when the child/children leave to build their own homes or pursue their dreams and aspirations.

THE OTHER WOMAN

If you just got married and you're probably reading this book during your honeymoon, few days or few months after your wedding; please skip this sub heading and I sincerely wish from the depth of my heart that you do not have to contend for the love, attention and affection of your husband with a strange woman.

No woman wants to hear this. Most women dread this like a plague including those who talk and act as if they do not care. I do sincerely hope that no wife has to deal with this. This is more than the man just having sex. It is betrayal, breaking the vows you took to honour one another with your bodies. There is absolutely nothing honourable in cheating. Most women do not mind managing a 'not too wealthy 'man but once he starts cheating, it builds a kind of resentment in them and kills trust which is one of the things that a healthy marriage needs.

Husbands, let me speak to you first. It is possible to be faithful. Don't let people deceive you with lies that all married men cheat. As a Christian, do you remember the story of Prophet Elijah in the Bible in the book of 1 Kings 18:22?

He was telling God that he is the only prophet left who haven't bowed down to Baal. He was feeling discouraged but God told him that wasn't true and that there are seven thousand in Israel who haven't bowed down to Baal (I Kings 19:18). The next time discouragement sets in and you begin to feel you are the only one who is faithful to your wife, know that it isn't true. There are millions if not billions of other men who are faithful to their wives. Do not see it as being odd. Besides, what is odd in being faithful? It even shows a high moral standard, discipline and a sense of respect for God. The issues being unfaithful create isn't worth it.

A lot of married women live in denial when they see the signs and know that their husbands are cheating on them. They console themselves and say, "As far as he respects me and doesn't rub it on my face, I am cool with it." Let us tell ourselves the truth; cheating in itself shows that he doesn't respect you. It is not about consoling ourselves and acting like we don't care when we are already developing health issues because of this and wishing we can leave. Enough of the pretence! If our society doesn't frown at divorce and if our faith permits it, a lot of women would have walked out a long time ago. They are celebrating anniversaries upon anniversaries when in essence, they stopped being married in their mind a long time ago.

At this point, you're probably asking what do to do when you find out there is another woman or when you have caught your husband in the very act and he cannot deny it.

Let me state here that the suggestions I will be giving below is not a comprehensive list. Your case might be peculiar and will need a different approach that might not be listed here.

— **Talk to God**

If you have been following my Facebook articles on my Friday Dose Series, you would notice that I have always maintained that I am first of all a Christian before a certified marriage mentor and relationship coach. You might have other choices and will have to do other things and take other steps but this is the first thing I advise you to do. Why? You need to know the next step to take and ask the Holy Spirit for wisdom on how to handle it. A lot of people miss it when found in this situation as they do not have anyone to pour out their heart to.

You might eventually need the services of a marriage counsellor but before you decide on who to go to and make up your mind if you really want to talk to someone, you need to talk to God. If you have a relationship with Him, you would know that you can speak to Him at any time without delay. He is always with you and that's why I suggest this as the first step. More so, the Holy Spirit can direct you on who to see. There are a lot of marriage counsellors out there and you need to be directed to the right one.

Someone once told me that I hardly tell her anything about my marriage and I just laughed because I have someone I do run to, not necessarily because of any issue in my marriage but when I need help on how to handle a situation or want to hear a trusted person's view on something. She is a deaconess in my church. There are so many deaconesses; so why her? I wasn't even close to her when I needed guidance on a particular aspect in my marriage but I felt led to approach her and I did that.

One other reason you should talk to God is to know if it is more of a spiritual attack that needs you to wage spiritual warfare. Some men that behave like dogs, sleeping with everything in skirts, might be under a spell and most marriage mentors will not be able to help you out except the one that is also spiritual enough to sense it and advise you appropriately. You need to fight for your home on your knees. You might notice that the other woman is married with children and her husband is aware and doesn't seem to care. Sometimes, it is not normal. Your husband might have been threatened by her husband countless times but he doesn't seem bothered. You could have reported him to his parents, senior siblings and his pastor or spiritual leader. Everything about him is going down and he is okay with it. That should send you a signal that your husband needs spiritual help.

He might not even be happy about what he is doing. I remember the story of a man who was so promiscuous that a lot of people couldn't understand why. He had a beautiful and submissive wife. One day, she had to ask him why he cheats on her. In tears, she asked if there was something she was not doing right. She actually wanted a divorce. This man's waywardness was so bad that he was sleeping with some ladies in his place of worship. He told his wife he doesn't know what comes over him and needs her help to overcome that.

Thankfully, she decided to stay. She started praying for her husband binding the spirit of lust, strange women, and promiscuity amongst others. Today, that family is now a happy home and he has since renewed his vow. Some men are not under any spiritual attack. They chase strange women with clear eyes but others are not really happy and conscious about it. Remember, there are always two sides to a coin.

— Speak Out

Enough of people advising wives of cheating husbands to keep quiet; this is doing more harm than good. A lot of people are sick because people expect them to act as if it is absolutely normal and a norm for all married men to cheat. The first person you need to speak out to is your husband. Let him know that you are aware of the other woman especially if you caught him in the act. I wonder why we act as if all is well when you cannot concentrate at work any longer because of this, you snap at your child/ children, and have nervous breakdown. While it is true that speaking out to a cheating husband might not change anything, you are however doing this for your own good. Let him know that you do not like it. He will know that is the cause of your constant nagging, emotional trauma or mental health issue. Some men will automatically do away with the other woman once they know you are aware of it while for some, it will change nothing.

Keeping calm and acting as if all is well can push the man afar the more. I heard the story of a woman who got back home from work and caught her husband in bed with someone. She did nothing. She only locked the door behind them and waited for the other woman to run away. The man was trying to apologize and she acted as if all was well. The next day, she still wasn't saying anything about it. The man had to sneak out of the house and never returned until after a long while. In as much as some men do not expect her to create a scene by calling neighbours, disgracing the lady, dragging her out or cursing her, she would have spoken to her husband or shown that she doesn't like it. The man got scared that he might be murdered at night one day and ran for his dear life.

When marriage mentors or people advise you to keep calm, it doesn't mean taking it to the extreme. I don't know if he later went back to that marriage. Let him know that you know he is seeing another woman or women whether he would do something about it or not. It will help him understand why you do not glow with excitement any longer when he tells you that you are the only woman in his life. After speaking out and letting him know about it, depending on what his response is and how badly you are affected by the new development, you should know if you have to still see a counsellor or not. I said 'depending on his response' because he might be very sorry and sincerely ready to put an end to it. All he needs is your forgiving heart and willingness to walk with him as he repents of his mistakes and turns a new leaf. You are his wife and you should know when your husband is genuinely sorry and ready to change or already showing signs of change.

Let me state here that before speaking out, you must be very sure that your husband is actually having an affair and you are not just accusing him falsely.

— Avoid Confronting the Other Woman/Women

A lot of wives have lost their lives and others have been utterly disgraced. I know a lot of young wives might argue with this but older wives will tell you the same thing. No matter how much you try to shift the whole blame to the other woman, your husband has the greatest fault. If you think he was charmed by the woman, it means he was careless about his spiritual life or careless about where he eats, as most charms these days from strange women are put in foods and drinks. That is why I do not encourage married men to keep eating from only one restaurant. You have eaten there until they know you as their regular customer and already know the particular meal you would order. This isn't good, not only for married men but for every one as well. It is also necessary to pray before eating meals outside.

Do you know that some men lie about their marital status? They deny being married and can swear. This is ridiculous.

By the way, how many women would you confront? If your husband is someone that fears what you can do to his mistress, he might leave her and move on to another one. So is that how you would be confronting different ladies around town?

Let me share this true life experience.

A lady shared her story of how her newly wedded husband of one year started chasing a particular lady and they started having an affair. On the night she found out, she was devastated. Her husband was sleeping and this lady sent a message to her husband's phone. She read it, went through other messages and almost fainted due to the content. She was so furious that she woke her husband up and created a scene. He didn't deny it and by morning, she was out to confront the other woman. The other woman was scared for her life and decided to keep off. However, her husband found another person; she discovered it again and repeated the same cycle. One day during her quiet time, it dawned on her that she would break down totally if she continued like that. She was already showing signs of a nervous breakdown. She decided to face her husband and forget the other women and that was the beginning of change in her home. She knew that it was not a spiritual attack because the women left her husband as soon as she confronted them.

Her husband needed to stop going out to look for them; it was as easy as that.

Do you know that some of these strange women are diabolical? You can go to confront them without being spiritually sound and they end up killing you and finally becoming the main woman. You need wisdom. Refuse to listen to people telling you to go to her house and beat her, create a scene or send bad boys after her. Going to her house is very dangerous. What if she locks you up there and harms you and no one even knows you went there?
It's degrading to fight with her in an open space. My dear, I know you are angry, upset and irritated depending on the damage she has caused in your home but please think about your safety. Most of those strange women have no shame and are not discreet in their affairs with married men. I am not trying to say those that are discreet about it are doing the right thing but a woman who isn't scared of the man's wife knowing her is a woman that is ready for anything. You can go and engage in a fight with her and she beats the hell out of you and tears your dress, leaving you naked. Some are so mean that they can run away with your phones and car keys, leaving you totally stranded and helpless. In this era of social media, you might wake up the next day and see your naked pictures on all social media platforms. Believe me, it is not worth it.

There was a young wife who went to fight with her husband's mistress and was beaten badly. People took photographs and this strange woman posted them online for the whole world to see. Her husband was at work when he got called by his family members and friends to log into Facebook. After seeing his wife's nakedness everywhere, he went into hiding for days. Of course, he quickly put a call to his mistress and she took down the post but what happens to those pictures that have already been saved by people?

By all means, save yourself from this kind of embarrassment.

— **Do Not Make the Other Woman the Object of Your Attention**

I know you might be deep in thoughts and wondering what your husband saw in her. Ironically, she might not be as beautiful as you are. Deep down in your heart, you know she doesn't measure up to you in any way. It is not unusual to find yourself checking out her pictures on all social media platforms as you try to solve the puzzle in your head and answer the big question, "Why her?"

You need to take hold of your thoughts and refuse to make her the centre of your life and the totality of discussion with your husband. It is enough that she is already causing issues in your home; do not let her occupy your mind.

Try to have a conversation with your husband without bringing her into it. If you need him to do something for you, simply state it without saying, "If it's your foolish mistress, you would have done it without her asking." Let her not affect your self-esteem and confidence. I know it might be difficult initially but you can do anything you put your mind to.

— Don't Become a Shadow of Yourself

Refuse to become a shadow of yourself because of this. Don't see yourself as a failure. Bear it in mind that not all men who cheat do that because of any fault of their wives or her inadequacies. It only takes a man who truly loves God to be faithful. If you are falling into a state of depression, seek help immediately. If you are developing any health challenge as a result of this, see a doctor and follow their recommendation closely. Don't be afraid to speak out to someone you trust.

— Look Within Yourself

I decided to write this as the last point so that it can sink deeply. Most times, we are good at shifting the blame and taking none of it. It is possible that some things you are doing or aren't doing pushes your spouse away from you. I do not know you and so I cannot tell you what things you are doing but I can only generally talk about some things that can push men out: a domineering wife, a nagging wife, a dirty wife, an incorrigible wife, a wife that denies her husband sex always, a wife that argues more than the chief judge and makes the home look like a courtroom, a wife that disrespects his parents and family.

You need to tell yourself the truth and ask deep questions that only you can answer. Did I give room for the entrance of the other woman because of my attitude? Has my husband been complaining about so many things I have been doing lately? When last did I satisfy my husband sexually? Have I put our marriage last while I put my job and other things aside God first? Ask yourself series of questions. Only you can give the answers to those questions above and others you might want to add to the list.

Don't get me wrong. I am not saying a man must cheat because of the reasons above. My point is, some men can be pushed out because of some of the reasons above and like I stated earlier on, the entrance of the other woman might also have nothing to do with you. I am only saying it is also advisable to look within as well. The steps listed above are NOT the only ways to deal with the other woman or man. You can also do what you know might work better for you. This is only a guide.

Also, this is in no way trying to encourage cheating among couples. It is in no way an outright license for men/women to cheat and come back apologizing. As Christians, cheating should not be heard of. This is why it's crucial to make up your mind right from your single days that infidelity would never be heard of in your home. Be disciplined enough to respect God and your spouse. Unfortunately, adultery is one of the most disturbing issues in marriages these days, even among Christians, which shouldn't be so.

Love Birds Exercise 7.

• Did you get married with the notion that what happens in marriage remains there? If yes, has this chapter helped in changing that notion?

• With all that has been happening in your life lately and the points listed in this chapter, do you think you need to reach out for help?

• If your answer to question 2 is yes, are you willing to do that individually or as a couple?

• Can you both discuss areas that have pushed you two further apart from each other?

• Make up your mind to love God enough not to cheat on your spouse.

AFTERWORD

Having established the fact that after the wedding ceremony comes the main marriage and that new couples must be willing to adjust to a new life/status after marriage, it is wisdom to be determined to make your marriage work. In as much as there is no exact manual for marriage, there are some things that can kill joy in marriage such as comparison, infidelity, wrong communication pattern and the like. Be sensitive.

Marriage is not a cult; so you must know when to reach out for help and speak to a trained, professional and Christian marriage counsellor. I sincerely pray that you enjoy your marriage. Together, let's change the narrative of marriage being a scam and that all married people are unhappy in their marriages. Marriage is a beautiful thing.

A LETTER FROM HER TO HIM

My adorable husband, the one I call my love and king. Yes, you are my earthly king.

I grew up with a single parent and I didn't really look forward to marriage because I felt true love doesn't exist. As a matter of fact, I only got married because that was expected of me, especially in Africa where marriage is still seen as a lady's greatest achievement. I am happy that this wrong notion is gradually changing.

I saw the way you treated me with utmost love and respect after our wedding and felt it was because we just got married. Somewhere deep inside my heart, I kept expecting the worst home but the worst hasn't come and hey, I don't ever want it to come.

You've taught me how to love by the way you love me. I loved you before we got married but I can boldly say I love you more now. Sometimes, I wonder if this is real. I only hope my heart doesn't burst open because it beats for only you. I never knew I was capable of loving someone this much.

Thank you for always helping out in the house. I might not say it often but I do appreciate it, especially when you serve me breakfast in bed.

I might not be perfect. However, I will try my best to make sure I constantly work towards being perfect. I can't wait for God to bless us with his heritage and I promise to be the best mother ever to them. Don't worry, they won't take your place.

One of the things that attracted me to you was your genuine love for God. Can you remember when we were planning our marriage and you still had to fulfil the financial vow you made to God? This touched me as I knew God will always come first in our home and I am very okay with that.

Most times, I pretend to be sleeping and I listen to you pray for me and our unborn children. Secretly, I ask myself how I got this lucky to have you.

I've watched you sleep several times and tears roll down my eyes as I thank God for the gift of you. You are everything I prayed and waited for.

I love you baby. You're the best gift from God after the gift of His only begotten son.
Let's keep serving God, ourselves and honouring the vow we exchanged. I know my job requires me meeting a lot of

people but believe me those men will never take your place in my life.

Correct me in love and tolerate my excesses while I also work on them. I will be everything this woman can possibly be.

With love,
Your darling wife.

Footnote: Wives, learn to write love letters to your husband frequently.

A LETTER FROM HIM TO HER

Dearest wife,

I've watched you become choked up with so many things lately. I have come to understand the strength of a woman. I also promise to help out in the house as often as I can.

I look at you and I am more convinced that I made the right choice though you make me feel I made a mistake especially when you are mad at me and threaten a divorce. Honey, I want you to know that we're in this together. None of us is leaving, I know you don't mean the words you say as you always come back to my arms later and give me a warm kiss, telling me you only needed my attention and that threat always does the magic for you.

I want you to stop threatening me with that before the devil takes advantage of it. I accept that I haven't always been there for you. I am always busy trying to make ends meet, make sure we have a roof over our head and try to save up before our little treasures from heaven arrive.

I promise to change and try my best to spend more time with you. I've discovered that quality time is your love language and I will start spending more time with you.

Nevertheless, know that I won't be perfect at all but I will try my best.

I have decided to always go on a yearly vacation with you. It might not be a very beautiful and spectacular place but having you by my side during those vacations will be the most beautiful and spectacular thing.

I know you want me to be the spiritual head of our home and that melts my heart. I love it when you tell me you want God to be first in our home.

Baby, I'm still a work in progress and with God in our boat, we will keep growing beyond leaps and bounds in this marriage.

I will love you faithfully and forever plus a day more.

Correct me in love when I go wrong. Don't scream or shout. No man loves that. Cut down the excuses each time we want to make love. When you give those constant excuses, it makes me feel you don't want to bond with me.

I also want you to trust me more. I haven't given you any reason to doubt me. When you act as if I have given you a reason to do so by constantly wanting to find out where and who I am with, it makes me feel my effort at honouring our marriage vows isn't appreciated. Baby, you have no rival. I want our children to look at us and know the qualities to look out for in their future spouse.

I don't know what life might throw at us and I sincerely wish it would be only things we can handle. A lot of things might change as we grow older together but my love and adoration for you will remain forever and a day more.

I love you, my wife. Thank you for accepting to walk this journey of forever with me. I love the way you call me baby.

With love,
Your darling husband.

Footnote: Husbands, learn to write love letters to your wife frequently.

WORK WITH ME

In my job as a relationship consultant and certified marriage coach, I can only admit that marriage is one of the most important journeys anyone can embark on.

If you're single, be sure you read my first book under relationship category titled, Before You Get Married.

Follow me on Facebook@**Ody Bassey Agbor** to get inspired by my free Friday Dose Series. There are lots of programs I anchor including Singles Raw Talk, Love Birds Masterclass, Marriage Consulting among others which come in different packages.

If you're married, you deserve the best marital relationship. If you are single, congratulations! You have an opportunity to prepare for a good marriage.

Would you like us to talk?
Connect with me.
Email: adede.bassey@yahoo.com
Phone: 07055239897 (WhatsApp Only)

ABOUT THE AUTHOR

Ody Adede Agbor is a lecturer in Elder Oyama Memorial College of Education, Obubra, Cross River State. She holds a B.sc (hons) in Sociology from University of Calabar, Nigeria and Masters in Marketing Communications from the prestigious Middlesex University, United Kingdom. She hails from Cross River in Nigeria. She is a registered member of Nigerian Institute of Management (NIM).

She is a certified marriage mentor and relationship coach with certification from The Institute for Marriage and Family Affairs (TIMFA) U.S.A. and also an Amazon Number One BestSelling Author of the book, Before You Get Married.

She's an advocate for healthy relationships and passionately counsels singles on marriage. Having worked with youths in her church and place of work, she knows how much of a struggle it is for them to maintain healthy relationships.

 She is the anchor of the inspiring Show, Singles RawTalk where she addresses issues that need to be tackled before singles walk down the aisle. Through writing and speaking, she inspires them to prepare for the responsibilities that come with being a husband or wife.

She runs a weekly series tagged, Friday Dose with Ody, which features inspiring articles with more focus on relationship and marriage issues for her audience.

She has been featured on several platforms including BEWA Interview Series, Radio Shows among others where she shared valuable lessons related to love, relationship and marriage.

She is happily married to Mr. Matthew Agbor.